How to Start & Manage a Convenience Food Store Business

A Practical Way to Start Your Own Business

by Jer̶r̶ Renn

How to Start & Manage
A Convenience Food Store Business

Lewis & Renn Associates, Inc.
Business & Professional Publishing
10315 Harmony Drive
Interlochen, Michigan 49643
(231) 275-7287

Leslie D. Renn
President

Jerre G. Lewis
Secretary-Treasurer

ISBN # 978-1-57916-184-2
Library of Congress Catalog Card Number
99-094181

TABLE OF CONTENTS

Chapter 1

Introduction

Selecting the right Convenience Food Store business opportunity requires careful, thorough evaluations of yourself. Owning your own business is as much a part of the American dream as owning a home, and for you, this urge represents one of life's most exciting challenges. This book is for those men and women who someday may go into business for themselves and for those who are already in business for themselves but wish to strengthen their entrepreneurial and managerial skills.

Entrepreneurs come in all shapes and sizes, personalities, and lifestyles. They are usually highly motivated, hard-working individuals who receive satisfaction from taking risks. Your business should interest you, not just be an income generator. Analyze your personal style. Do you like working with people? Are you a self starter, goal oriented, persistent, a risk taker, willing to work hard and long hours?

If you have been honest in evaluating yourself, you will now select the right type of business. Before you can determine which of the multitude of businesses is right for you to start, you must evaluate the businesses you want to start by asking these questions. Is the business area growing? How does the economy affect it? Who dominates its market? Once you have considered a business that satisfies your needs and interest you must prepare a formal business plan by following the outline given in this book.

Small businesses constitute a dynamic and critical sector of the U.S. economy. Every year in the United States more than 600,000 new businesses are launched by independent men and women eager to make their own decisions, express their own ideas, and be their own bosses. But running your own business is not as easy as it may seem. There can be problems with the inventory, or getting the right goods delivered on time. Yet, managing one's own business can be a personally and financially rewarding experience for an individual strong enough to meet the test. A person with stamina, maturity, and creativity, one who is willing to make sacrifices, may find making a go of a struggling enterprise an exhilarating challenge with many compensations.

Small business owners are a dedicated group of people who work hard and whose hours on the job usually exceed the nine-to-five routine. The owner's commitment is the key to many successful small businesses; an entrepreneur is able to communicate ideas, lead, plan, be patient, and work well with people.

Managing a business requires more than the possession of technical knowledge. Because most small businesses are started by technical people, such as engineers and salesmen, their managerial acumen is often less developed than their technical skills. The need to plan for management is common to every type of and size of business, and there are certain steps that must be taken. Although some of them are very elementary — such as applying for a city business permit — the most important are often complex and difficult and require the advice of specialists: accountants, attorneys, insurance brokers, and/or bankers. For almost any business though, the first step will be to translate the entrepreneur's basic idea into a concrete plan for action.

To gauge your level of entrepreneurial spirit, the following quiz was created. Please answer each question honestly and then total the columns.

ENTREPRENEURIAL QUIZ

	YES	NO	SOMETIMES
1. I am a self-starter. Nobody has to tell me how to get going.	____	____	_____
2. I am capable of getting along with just about everybody.	____	____	_____
3. I have no trouble getting people to follow my lead.	____	____	_____
4. I like to be in charge of things and see them through.	____	____	_____
5. I always plan ahead before beginning a project. I am usually the one who gets everyone organized.	____	____	_____
6. I have a lot of stamina. I can keep going as long as necessary.	____	____	_____
7. I have no trouble making decisions and can make up my mind in a hurry.	____	____	_____
8. I say exactly what I mean. People can trust me.	____	____	_____
9. Once I make my mind up to do something, nothing can stop me.	____	____	_____
10. I am in excellent health and have a lot of energy.	____	____	_____

	YES	NO	SOMETIMES

11. I have experience or technical knowledge in the business I intend to start.

       ____   ____   _____

12. I feel comfortable taking risks if it is something I really believe in.

       ____   ____   _____

13. I have good communication skills.

       ____   ____   _____

14. I am flexible in my dealings with people and situations.

       ____   ____   _____

15. I consider myself creative and resourceful.

       ____   ____   _____

16. I can analyze a situation and take steps to correct problems.

       ____   ____   _____

17. I think I am capable of maintaining a good working relationship with employees.

       ____   ____   _____

18. I am not a dictator. I am willing to listen to employees, customers and suppliers.

       ____   ____   _____

19. I am not rigid in my policies. I am willing to adjust to meet the needs of employees, customers, and suppliers.

       ____   ____   _____

20. More than anything else, I want to run my own business.

       ____   ____   _____

Total of Column #1   _____

Total of Column #2   _____

Total of Column #3   _____

If the total of Column #1 is the highest, then you will probably be very successful in running your own business.

If the total of Column #2 is the highest, you may find that running a business is more than you can handle.

If the total of Column #3 is the highest, you should consider taking on a partner who is strong in your weak areas.

NOTE: This quiz was adapted from the Small Business Administration publication *Checklist for Going Into Business.*

Notes

Chapter 2

Planning the Business

The Dream of self-employment can be fulfilled. You don't need to finance the opening of an elaborate office or facility to start your own one-person corporation either. You can start your own Convenience Food Store business.

Anyone preparing to run an Convenience Food Store business needs to learn a great deal to assure the best possible chance for success.

GETTING STARTED

The following is a list of what you need to accomplish to insure that your Convenience Food Store endeavor will head in the right direction.

1. Define your educational background and work experience.

2. Survey all the basic types of Convenience Food Store businesses.

3. Define what products or services your Convenience Food Store business will be marketing.

4. Define who will be using your products/services.

5. Define why they will be purchasing your products/services.

6. List all competitors in your Convenience Food Store marketing area.

ZONING REGISTRATIONS

Convenience Food Store businesses are subject to many laws and regulations enforced by state, county, township governmental units. Most jurisdictions now have codes, a zoning board, and an appeal board which regulate businesses. Areas often are zoned residential, commercial or industrial.

You must become familiar with these regulations. If you are doing business in violation of these regulations, you could be issued a cease and desist order or fined.

Certain kinds of goods cannot be produced in the home, though these restrictions vary somewhat from state-to-state. Most states outlaw home production of fireworks, drugs, poisons, explosives, sanitary/medical products and some toys.

Many localities have registration requirements for new businesses. You will need to obtain a work certificate or license from the state.

TAX REQUIREMENTS

<u>Application for Employer Identification Number</u>, Form SS-4. This registers you with the Internal Revenue Service as a business. If you have employees, you should ask for Circular E along with your ID number. Circular E explains federal income and social security tax withholding requirements.

<u>Employer's Annual Unemployment Tax Return</u>, Form 940. This is only if you have employees. It's used to report and pay the Federal Unemployment Compensation Tax.

<u>Employee's Withholding Allowance Certificate</u>, W-4. Every employee must complete the W-4 so the proper amount of income tax can be withheld from the

employee's pay. If the employee claims more than 15 allowances or a complete withholding exemption while having a salary of more than $200 a week, a copy of the W-4 must go to the IRS.

Employer's Wage and Tax Statement, W-2. Used to report to the IRS the total taxes withheld and total compensation paid to each employee per year.

Reconciliation/Transmittal of Income and Tax Statements, W-3. Used to total all information from the W-2. Sent to the Social Security Administration.

The IRS puts on monthly workshops on understanding and using these forms. Call your local IRS office for further information.

States also have various tax form requirements including: an unemployment tax form, a certificate of registration application, a sales and use tax return, an employer's quarterly contribution and payroll report, an income tax withholding registration form, an income tax withholding form, and others. Some forms apply only to employers who have employees. Your local IRS office and state Office of Taxation can provide you with listings of forms you will need to start your business. The following table outlines Federal tax form requirements.

Every small business begins with an idea — a product to be manufactured or sold, a service to be performed.

Whatever the business or its degree of complexity, the owner needs a business plan in order to transform a vision into a working operation.

This business plan should describe in writing and in figures the proposed Convenience Food Store business and its products, services, or manufacturing processes. It should also include an analysis of the market, a marketing strategy, an organizational plan, and measurable financial objectives.

WHAT SHOULD A BUSINESS PLAN COVER?

It should be a thorough and objective analysis of both personal abilities and business requirements for a particular product or service. It should define strategies for such functions as marketing and production, organization and legal aspects, accounting and finance. A business plan should answer such questions as:

What do I want and what am I capable of doing?

What are the most workable ways of achieving my goals?

What can I expect in the future?

There is no single best way to begin. What follows is simply a guide and can be changed to suit individual needs.

1. Define Long-term goals.
2. State short-term.
3. Set marketing strategies to meet goals and objectives.
4. Analyze available resources.
5. Assemble financial data.
6. Review plan.

Please refer to Figure 2.1 for a complete business plan outline.

The business operator with a realistic plan has the best chance for success.

Figure 2.1

BUSINESS PLAN FOR SMALL BUSINESSES

    I.   Type of Business

    II.   Location

    III.   Target Market

    IV.   Planning Process

    V.   Organizational Structure

    VI.   Staffing Procedures

    VII.   Market Strategy

    IX.   Financial Planning

    X.   Budgeted Balance Sheet

    XI.   Budgeted Income Statement

    XII.   Budgeted Cash Flow Statement

    XIII.   Break-Even Chart

Notes

Chapter 3

Marketing Strategies
for an Convenience Food Store Business

As a potential Convenience Food Store business owner, it is important to learn all you can about marketing. You will need to know how to identify your market and how to market your product or service.

As a business person who looks for a profit from the sale of goods, you recognize that without people who want to buy, there is no demand for the things you want to sell. Thus, it is important that, in addition to knowing about the functions of marketing, you also study the activities that will influence the consumer. When you satisfy the specific needs and wants of the customer, then he or she may be willing to pay you a price that will include a profit for you — and to make a profit is one of the reasons you have become an Convenience Food Store business owner. Although there are many activities connected with marketing, most of them can be classified in these categories: buy, finance, transport, standardize, store, insure, advertise and sell.

Target Market Analysis

Before you can create a successful marketing campaign, it's necessary to determine your target market (toward whom to direct your energies). The whole concept of target marketing can seem very scary at first. On the surface, targeting appears to be limiting the scope of the pool of potential customers. Many people fear that by defining a market, they will lose business. They are concerned that they will choose the wrong market. Or that other practitioners will take just anybody and therefore some of their business.

You must keep in mind that the purpose of defining your target market is to make your life easier and increase the productivity of your promotional endeavors. Many opportunities exist in this world and it's impossible to pursue them all or be everything to everyone. You need to know where to focus your energy and money when it comes to promotion and advertising.

The two most common means of market analysis are demographics and psychographics, which describe a person in terms of objective data and personality attributes.

Demographics are statistics such as:
- age
- gender
- income level
- geographic location
- occupation
- education level

Psychographics are lifestyle factors including:
- special interest activities
- philosophical beliefs
- social factors
- cultural involvements

The more you know about your potential customers, the easier it is to develop an appropriate position statement and design an effective marketing campaign. The actual number of target markets you have depends mainly upon the size of your practice and the scope of your knowledge.

Your Target Market Profile

In order to clarify your target market(s) you need to delineate the demographic and psychographic factors and then identify the characteristics your customers have in common.

Describe your current customers and those who are most likely your future customers:

What is the age range and average age of your customers?

What is the percentage of males?

What is the percentage of females?

What is the average educational level of your customers?

Where do your customers live?

What are the occupations of your customers?

Where do your customers work?

What is the average annual income level of your customers?

Of what special interest groups are your customers members?

What is the primary reason your customers use your services?

Defining Your Target Market(s)

Write a descriptive statement for each of your target markets (refer to your "Target Market Profile"). Include a brief overview of the services you are providing to that group and a detailed analysis of the characteristics of the specific clientele.

Target Market 1:

Target Market 2:

Target Market 3:

Convenience Food Store Business Marketing

The foundation for creating a thriving customer base.

A. Overview

This section is about clarifying your beliefs and attitudes toward your profession and determining the image you wish to portray.

1. Describe the "character" that you want for your business. Depict the image you want to convey:

2. State your philosophy in regard to your business:

3. Describe your philosophy regarding your practice in business:

B. Customer Profile

This is a descriptive analysis of your current and potential customers — who they are, what their interests are, and where you can find them. Include each of your target markets.

1. Target Market 1:

2. Target Market 2:

3. Target Market 3:

C. Competition's Marketing Assessment

The first phase in planning your promotional campaign is appraising the competition. List each of your major competitors and describe the marketing strategies they utilize. Be certain to include where and how often they advertise.

1. Major Competitor 1:

2. Major Competitor 2:

3. Major Competitor 3:

4. Major Competitor 4:

5. Major Competitor 5:

6. Major Competitor 6:

Convenience Food Store Marketing Planning

Outline for Marketing:

    I. Produce/Service Concept
       A. Name of produce or service
       B. Descriptive characteristics of product or service
       C. Unit sales
       D. Analysis of market trends

    II. Number of Customers in Market Area:
       A. Profile of customers
       B. Average customer expenditure
       C. Total market

    III. Your Market Potential:
       A. Total market divided by competition
       B. Total market multiplied by percent who will buy your product

    IV. Needs of Customers:
       A. Identification
       B. Pleasure
       C. Social approval
       D. Personal interest
       E. Price

    V. Direct Marketing Sources:
       A. Trade magazines
       B. Trade associates
       C. Small Business Administration (SBA)
       D. Government publications
       E. Yellow Pages
       F. Marketing directories

    VI. Customer Profile:
       A. Geographical
       B. Gender
       C. Age range
       D. Income brackets
       E. Occupation
       F. Educational level

Chapter 4

Promoting the Convenience Food Store Business

When a new business is opened, the owner must be prepared to publicize the business or its chance for success will be slim. Only a few businesses — such as those with a prime location, nationally known name, or a built-in clientele — can succeed without advertising to promote market awareness and stimulate sales.

The first purpose — promoting customer awareness — applies as much to established businesses as to newcomers.

In the Convenience Food Store business, you will find it easier to retain old customers than to win new ones. When old customers move away from your area, or when their buying needs change, you need new customers to maintain your sales volume. If you expect your business to gain, you will need additional new customers. New customers are those who move into your area or who have grown into your line of products because now they can afford them or they need them. We see advertising and we hear advertising all around us, and yet that is only a part of it. Through advertising, you call the attention of customers to your products.

As a small business owner, you may advertise your business through your location. People pass by and are attracted to your operation because of what you are selling. To get a better idea of what advertising is, consider some of the following functions of advertising:

1. *To inform:* Letting customers know what you have for sale through brochures, leaflets, newspapers, radio, TV, and etc.

2. *Persuade:* Persuasion is the art of leading individuals to do what you want them to do. There are sales personnel who have persuasive sales presentations, but persuasion in advertising is nonpersonal. The appeal is made through the printed or spoken words or a picture. The influence of an ad on readers occurs as purchasers choose what they want among different products, and different wants. To gain the actions you want — a sale — you must persuade a customer to examine personally what you have for sale.

3. *Reminder:* Advertising performs it's third function when it reminds those who have been persuaded to buy once that the same product will bring satisfaction. The ad will also remind a customer of the characteristics of a product purchased some time ago, and where he or she bought it. Because customers change their loyalty to a place of business, their taste for products, and often their trading area patronage, advertising is necessary to draw new customers and to hold old customers. To generate results from advertising that will be profitable to your business, you will have to produce answers to the what, where and how of advertising.

What to Advertise

The nature of your business will partially answer the question "Shall I advertise goods or services?" What are the outstanding features of your business? Is it unique in any way? Does it have strong points? Do you have something to offer that the competition is not able to duplicate? Answers to these questions will give you a start in deciding what to advertise.

Where to Advertise

Of course, you will want to advertise within your marketing area, however there are a few guidelines to remember:

A. Who are your customers?

B. What is their income range?

C. Why do they buy?

D. How do they buy? Do they pay Cash? Charge?

E. What is the radius of your market area?

How to Advertise:

In determining how to advertise, you will have to consider your dollar allocation for advertising and the media suitable to your particular kind of business. However, it is important to have a balance between the presentation of the product or service being advertised and the application of three basic principles.

1. Gain the attention of the audience.

2. Establish a need.

3. Tell where that need may be filled.

See Figure A for an outline of the different advertising media and Figure B for budget on media goals.

Figure A

Advertising Media

Media	Market Coverage	Type of Audience
Daily Newspaper	Single community or entire metro area; zoned editions sometimes available	General
Weekly Newspaper	Single community	Residents
Telephone Directory	Geographical area or occupational field served by the directory	Active shoppers for goods or services
Direct mail audience	Controlled by the advertiser	Controlled
Radio audience	Definable market area	Selected
Television audience	Definable market area	Various
Outdoor	Entire metro area	General auto drivers
Magazine	Entire metro area or magazine region	Selected audience

Figure A

Promotion and Advertising Plan — Convenience Food Store Business

In designing your promotional plan, it's wise to use a variety of media. You must have specific goals, time lines and budgets for each marketing application

Media	Goal	Timeline	Budget

Notes

Chapter 5

Financial Planning for an Convenience Food Store Business

Financial planning is the process of analyzing and monitoring the financial performance of your business so you can assess your current position and anticipate future problem areas. The daily, monthly, seasonal, and yearly operation of your business requires attention to the figures that tell you about the firm's financial health.

Maintaining good financial records is a necessary part of doing business.

The increasing number of governmental regulations alone makes it virtually impossible to avoid keeping detailed records. Just as important is to keep them for yourself. The success of your business depends on them. An efficient system of record keeping can help you to:

- make management decisions
- compete in the marketplace
- monitor performance
- keep track of expenses
- eliminate unprofitable merchandise
- protect your assets
- prepare your financial statements

Financial skills should include understanding of the balance sheet, the profit-and-loss statement, cash flow projection, break-even analysis, and source and application of funds. In many businesses, the husband and wife run the business; it is especially important that both of them understand financial management. Most small business owners are not accountants, but they must understand the tool of financial management if they are going to be able to measure the return on their investment. Although good records are essential to good financial planning, they alone are not enough because their full use requires interpretation and analysis. The owner/manager's financial decisions concerning return on invested funds, approaches to banks, securing greater supplier credit, raising additional equity capital and so forth, can be more successful if he takes the time to develop understanding and use of the balance sheet and profit-and-loss statement.

Balance Sheet:

The balance sheet, Figure I, shows the financial condition of a business at the end of business on a specific day. It is called a balance sheet because the total assets balance with, or are equal to, total liabilities plus owner's capital balance. Current assets are those that the owner does not anticipate holding for long. This category includes cash, finished goods in inventory, and accounts receivable. Fixed assets are long-term assets, including plant and equipment. A third possible category is the intangible asset of goodwill. Liabilities are debts owed by the business, including both accounts payable, which are usually short-term, and notes payable, which are usually long-term debts such as mortgage payments. The difference between the value of the assets and the value of the liabilities is the capital. This category includes funds invested by the owner plus accumulated profits, less withdrawals.

The Income Statement:

This statement, Figure II, is also known as a profit-and loss (P&L) statement. It shows how a business has performed over a certain period of time. An income statement specifies sales, costs of sales, gross profit, expenses and net income or loss from operations.

Figure I

Financial Forecast

Opening Balance Sheet - Date

ASSETS

Current Assets

Cash and bank accounts		$	
Accounts receivable		$	
Inventory		$	
Other current assets		$	
TOTAL CURRENT ASSETS	(A)	$	

Fixed Assets

Property owned		$	
Furniture and equipment		$	
Business automobile		$	
Leasehold improvements		$	
Other fixed assets		$	
TOTAL FIXED ASSETS	(B)	$	
TOTAL ASSETS	(A+B = X)	$	

LIABILITIES

Current Liabilities (due within the next 12 months)

Bank loans		$	
Other loans		$	
Accounts payable		$	
Other current liabilities		$	
TOTAL CURRENT LIABILITIES	(C)	$	

Long-term Liabilities

Mortgages		$	
Long-term loans		$	
Other long-term liabilities		$	
TOTAL LONG-TERM LIABILITIES	(D)	$	
TOTAL LIABILITIES	(C+D = Y)	$	
NET WORTH	(X-Y = Z)	$	
TOTAL NET WORTH AND LIABILITIES	(Y+Z)	$	

Figure II

Business Income and Expense Forecast for the Next 12 Months

One year estimate ending _____ , 19 _____

Projected Number of Clients

For your services _____

For your products _____

TOTAL NUMBER OF CLIENTS _____

Projected Income

Sessions $_____

Product sales $_____

Other $_____

TOTAL INCOME $_____

Projected Expenses

Start-up costs $_____

Monthly expenses (x 12) $_____

Annual expenses $_____

TOTAL EXPENSES $_____

TOTAL OPERATING PROFIT (OR LOSS) $_____

CAPITAL REQUIRED FOR THE NEXT 12 MONTHS $_____

Convenience Food Store Business

Start-Up Costs Worksheet	
Item	**Estimated Expense**
Open checking account	$
Telephone installation	$
Equipment	$
First & last month's rent, security deposit, etc.	$
Supplies	$
Business cards, stationery, etc.	$
Advertising and promotion package	$
Decorating and remodeling	$
Furniture and fixtures	$
Legal and professional fees	$
Insurance	$
Utility deposits	$
Beginning inventory	$
Installation of fixtures and equipment	$
Licenses and permits	$
Other	$
TOTAL	$

Fixed Annual Expense Worksheet	
Item	**Estimated Expense**
Property insurance	$
Business auto insurance	$
Licenses and permits	$
Liability insurance	$
Disability insurance	$
Professional society membership	$
Fees (legal, accounting, etc.)	$
Taxes	$
Other	$
TOTAL	$

Monthly Business Expense Worksheet		
Expense	**Estimated Monthly Cost**	**X 12**
Rent	$	$
Utilities	$	$
Telephone	$	$
Bank fees	$	$
Supplies	$	$
Stationery and business cards	$	$
Networking club dues	$	$
Education (seminars, books professional journals, etc.)	$	$
Business car (Payments, gas, repairs, etc)	$	$
Advertising and promotion	$	$
Postage	$	$
Entertainment	$	$
Repair, cleaning and maintenance	$	$
Travel	$	$
Business loan payments	$	$
Salary/Draw	$	$
Staff salaries	$	$
Miscellaneous	$	$
Taxes	$	$
Professional fees	$	$
Decorations	$	$
Furniture and fixtures	$	$
Equipment	$	$
Inventory	$	$
Other	$	$
TOTAL MONTHLY	$	$
TOTAL YEARLY		$

	January Estimate	January Actual	February Estimate	February Actual	March Estimate	March Actual
Cash Flow Forecast						
Beginning cash						
Plus monthly income from: Fees						
Sales						
Loans						
Other						
TOTAL CASH AND INCOME						
Expenses:						
Rent						
Utilities						
Telephone						
Bank fees						
Supplies						
Stationery and business cards						
Insurance						
Dues						
Education						
Auto						
Advertising and promotion						
Postage						
Entertainment						

Cash Flow Forecast (Continued)						
	January Estimate	January Actual	February Estimate	February Actual	March Estimate	March Actual
Repair and maintenance						
Travel						
Business loan payments						
Licenses and permits						
Salary/Draw						
Staff salaries						
Taxes						
Professional fees						
Decorations						
Furniture and fixtures						
Equipment						
Inventory						
Other Expenses						
TOTAL EXPENSES						
ENDING CASH (+/-)						

Notes

Chapter 6

Convenience Food Store Business Planning

Introduction

Our increasingly service oriented economy offers a widening spectrum of opportunities for customized and personalized small business growth. Though untrained entrepreneurs have traditionally had a high rate of failure, small businesses can be profitable. Success in a small Convenience Food Store business is not an accident. It requires both skills in a service or product area and acquisition of management and attitudinal competencies.

The purpose of this publication is to help you take stock of your interests, aptitudes and skills. Many people have good business ideas but not everyone has what it takes to succeed. If you are convinced that a profitable Convenience Food Store business is attainable, this publication will provide step-by-step guidance in development of the basic written business plan.

Information Gathering

A helpful tool for use in determining if you are ready to take the risks of an Convenience Food Store business operation is the SMA publication entitled *Going Into Business* (MP-12).

It will help you focus on the basic steps in information gathering and business planning.

Careful planning is required to research legal and tax issues, proper space utilization and to establish time management discipline. Inadequate or careless attention to development of a detailed business plan can be costly for you and your family in terms of lost time, wasted talent and disappearing dollars.

The Entrepreneurial Personality

A variety of experts have documented research that indicates that successful small business entrepreneurs have some common characteristics. How do you measure up? On this checklist, write a "Y" if you believe the statement describes you; a "N" if it doesn't; and a "U" if you can't decide:

_____ I have a strong desire to be my own boss.

_____ Win lose or draw, I want to be master of my own financial destiny.

_____ I have significant specialized business ability based on both my education and my experience.

_____ I have an ability to conceptualize the whole of a business; not just its individual parts, but how they relate to each other.

_____ I develop an inherent sense of what is "right" for a business and have the courage to pursue it.

_____ One or both of my parents were entrepreneurs; calculate risk-taking runs in the family.

_____ My life is characterized by a willingness and capacity to preserver.

_____ I possess a high level of energy, sustainable over long hours to make the business successful.

While not every successful Convenience Food Store business owner starts with a "Y" answer to all of these questions, three or four "N"s and "U"s should be sufficient reason for you to stop and give a second thought to going it alone. Many proprietors who sense entrepreneurial deficiencies seek extra training a support their limitations with help from a skilled team of business advisors such as accountants, bankers and attorneys.

Selecting a Business

A logical first step for the undecided is to list potential areas of personal background, special training, education and job experience, and special interests that could be developed into a business. Review the following list of activities which have proven marketable for others. On a scale of "0" (no interest or strength) to "10" (maximum interest or strength) indicate the potential for you and a total score for each activity.

Time Management

For both the novice and the experienced business person planning a small Convenience Food Store enterprise, an early concern requiring self-evaluation is time management.

It is very difficult for some people to make and keep work schedules even in a disciplined office setting. As your own boss the problem can be much greater. To determine how much time you can devote to your business, begin by drafting a weekly task timetable listing all current and potential responsibilities and the blocks of time required for each. When and how can business responsibilities be added without undue physical or mental stress on you or your family? Potential conflicts must be faced and resolved at the outset and as they occur, otherwise your business can become a nightmare. During the first year of operation, continue to chart, post and checkoff tasks on a daily, weekly and monthly basis.

Distractions and excuses for procrastination abound. It is important to keep both a planning and operating log. These tools will help avoid oversights and provide vital information when memory fails.

To improve the quality of work time, consider installation of a telephone line for the business and attaching an answering machine to take messages when you do not wish to be distracted or are away from your business. A business line has the added advantage of allowing you to have a business listing in the phone book and if you wish to buy it, an ad in the classified directory.

Is an Convenience Food Store Business Site Allowable?

Now you will want to investigate potential legal and community problems associated with operating the business. You should gather, read and digest specialized information concerning federal, state, county and municipal laws and regulations concerning Convenience Food Store business operations.

Check first! Get the facts in writing. Keep a topical file for future reference. Some facts and forms will be needed for your business plan. There may be limitations enforced that can make your planned business impossible or require expensive modifications to your property.

Items to be investigated, recorded and studied are:

TO DO   DONE

_____   _____   county or city zoning code restrictions
_____   _____   necessary permits and licenses for operation
_____   _____   state and local laws and codes regarding zoning
_____   _____   deed or lease restrictions such as covenants and
                     restrictive conditions of purchase

_____	_____	parking and customer access; deliveries
_____	_____	sanitation, traffic and noise codes
_____	_____	signs and advertising
_____	_____	state and federal code requirements for space, ventilation, heat and light
_____	_____	limitations on the number and type of workers. If not, check with the local Chamber of Commerce office
_____	_____	reservations that neighbors may have about a business next to or near them

Here are some ways to collect your information. Call or visit the zoning office at county headquarters or city hall. In some localities the city or county Office of Economic Development has print materials available to pinpoint key "code" items affecting a business.

Even in rural areas, the era of unlimited free enterprise is over. Although the decision makers may be in the state capital or in a distant regional office of a federal agency, check before investing in inventory, equipment or marketing programs. If in doubt, call the state office of Industrial Development or the nearest SBA district office. In some states the county agent or home demonstration agent will have helpful information concerning rural or farm business development.

Is the Business Site Insurable?

In addition to community investigations, contact your insurance company or agent. It is almost certain that significant changes will be required in your coverage and limits when you start a business. When you have written a good description of your business, call your agent for help in insuring you properly against new hazards resulting from your business operations such as:

- Fire, theft and casualty damage to inventories and equipment
- business interruption coverage
- fidelity bonds for employees
- liability for customers, vendors and others visiting the business
- workmen's compensation
- group health and life insurance
- product liability coverage if you make or sell a product; workmanship liability for services
- business use of vehicle coverage

Overall Convenience Food Store Site Evaluation

After you have gathered as much information as seems practical you may wish to evaluate several different locations. Here's a handy checklist. Using the "0" to "10" scale, grade these vital factors:

Factors to Consider

Factor	Grades 0-10
1. Customer convenience	_____
2. Availability of merchandise or raw materials	_____
3. Nearby competition	_____
4. Transportation availability and rates	_____
5. Quality and quantity of employees available	_____
6. Availability of parking facilities	_____

7. Adequacy of utilities (sewer, water, power, gas) _____

8. Traffic flow _____

9. Tax burden _____

10. Quality of police and fire services _____

11. Environmental factors _____

12. Physical suitability for future expansion _____

13. Provision for future expansion _____

14. Vendor delivery access _____

15. Personal convenience _____

16. Cost of operation _____

17. Other factors including how big you get without moving _____

TOTALS _____

Writing the Business Plan

Now that your research and plan development is nearing completion, it is time to move into action. If you are still in favor of going ahead, it is time to take several specific steps. The key one is to organize your dream scheme into a business plan.

What is it?

- As a business plan it is written by the Convenience Food Store business owner with outside help as needed
- It is accurate and concise as a result of careful study
- It explains how the business will function in the marketplace
- It clearly depicts its operational characteristics
- It details how it will be financed
- It outlines how it will be managed
- It is the management and financial "blueprint" for start-up and profitable operation
- It serves as a prospectus for potential investors and lenders

Why create it?

- The process of putting the business plan together, including the thought that you put in before writing it, forces you to take an objective, critical, unemotional look at your entire business proposal
- The finished written plan is an operational tool which, when properly used, will help you manage your business and work toward its success
- The completed business plan is a means for communicating your ideas to others and provides the basis for financing your business

Who should write it?

- The Convenience Food Store owner to the extend possible
- Seek assistance in weak areas, such as:
    - accounting
    - insurance
    - capital requirements
    - operational forecasting
    - tax and legal requirements

When should a business plan be used?
- To make crucial start-up decisions
- To reassure lenders or backers
- To measure operations progress
- To test planning assumptions
- As a basis for adjusting forecasts
- To anticipate ongoing capital and cash requirements
- As the benchmark for good operations management

Proposed Outline for Convenience Food Store Business Plan

This outline is suggested for a small proprietorship or family business. Shape it to fit *your* unique needs. For more complex manufacturing or franchise operations see the Resource section for other options.

Part I - Business Organization

Cover page:

    A.   Business name:

            Street address:

            Mailing address:

            Telephone number:

            Owner(s) name(s):

Inside pages:

    B.   Business form:

            (proprietorship, partnership, corporation)

            If incorporated (state incorporation)

            Include copies of key subsidiary documents in an appendix.

Remember even partnerships require written agreements of terms and conditions to avoid later conflicts and to establish legal entities and equities. Corporations require charters, articles of incorporation and bylaws.

Part II - Business Purpose and Function

In this section, write an accurate yet, concise description of the business. Describe the business you plan to start in narrative form.

What is the principal activity? Be specific. Give product or service description(s):

- retail sales?

- manufacturing?

- service?

- other?

How will it be started?

- a new start up

- the expansion of an existing business

- purchase of a going business

- a franchise operation

- actual or projected start up date

Why will it succeed? Promote your idea!

- how and why this business will be successful

- what is unique about your business

- what is its market "niche"

What is your experience in this business? If you have a current resume of your career, include it in an appendix and reference it here. Otherwise write a narrative here and include a resume in the finished product. If you lack specific experience, detail how you plan to gain it, such as training, apprenticeship or working with partners who have experience.

The Marketing Plan

The marketing plan is the core of your business rationale. To develop a consistent sales growth an Convenience Food Store business person much become knowledgeable about the market. To demonstrate your understanding, this section of the Convenience Food Store business plan should seek to concisely answer several basic questions:

Who is your market?
- Describe the profile of your typical customer

   Age?

   Male, female, both?

   How many in family?

   Annual family income?

   Location?

   Buying patterns?

   Reason to buy from you?

Other?

- Biographically describe your trading area (i.e., county, state, national)

- Economically describe your trading area: (single family, average earnings, number of children)

How large is the market?

- Total units or dollars?

- Growing ____ Steadily ____ Decreasing ____

- If growing, annual growth rate. _____

Who is your competition?

No small business operates in a vacuum. Get to know and respect the competition. Target your marketing plans. Identify direct competitors (both in terms of geography and product lines), and those who are similar or marginally comparative. Begin by listing names, addresses and products or service. Detail briefly but concisely the following information concerning each of your competitors:

- Who are the nearest ones?

- How are their businesses similar or competitive to yours?

- Do you have a unique "niche"? Describe it.

- How will your service or product be better or more saleable than your competitors?

- Are their businesses growing? Stable? Declining? Why?

- What can be learned from observing their operations or talking to their present or former clients?

- Will you have competitive advantages or disadvantages? Be honest!

What percent of the market will you penetrate?

1. estimate the market in total units or dollars

2. estimate your planned volume

3. amount your volume will add to total market

4. subtract 3 from 2

Item 4 represents the amount of your planned volume that must be taken away from the competition.

What pricing and sales terms are you planning?

The primary consideration in pricing a product or service is the value that it represents to the customer. If, on the previous checklist of features, your product is truly ahead of the field, you can command a premium price. On the other hand, if it is a "me too" product, you may have to "buy" a share of the market to get your foothold and then try to move price up later. This is always risky and difficult. One rule will always hold: ultimately, the market will set the price. If your selling price does not exceed your costs and expenses by the margin necessary to keep your business healthy, you will fail. Know your competitors pricing policies. Send a friend to comparison shop. Is there discounting? Special sales? Price leaders? Make some "blind" phone calls. Detail your pricing policy.

What is your sales plan?

Describe how you will sell, distribute or service what you sell. Be specific. Below are outlined some common practices:

Direct Sales - by telephone or in person. The tremendous growth of individual sales representatives who sell by party bookings, door to door, and through distribution of call back promotional campaigns suggests that careful research is required to be profitable.

Mail Order - Specialized markets for leisure time or unique products have grown as more two income families find less time to shop. Be aware of recent mail order legislation and regulation.

Franchising -

a. You may decide to either buy into someone else's franchise as a franchisee, or

b. Create your own franchise operation that sells rights to specific territories or product lines to others. Each will require further legal, financial and marketing research.

Management Plan

Who will do what?

Be sure to include four basic sets of information:

1. State a personal history of principals and related work, hobby or volunteer experience (include formal resumes in Appendix)

2. List and describe specific duties and responsibilities of each

3. List benefits and other forms of compensation for each

46

4. Identify other professional resources available to the business: Example: Accountant, lawyer, insurance broker, banker. Describe relationship of each to business: Example "Accountant available on part-time hourly basis, as needed, initial agreement calls for services not to exceed x hours per month at $xx.xx per hour."

To make this section graphically clear, start with a simple organizational chart that lists specific tasks and shows, *who* (type of person is more important than an individual name other than for principals) will do *what* indicate by arrows, work flow and lines of responsibility and/or communications. Consider the following examples:

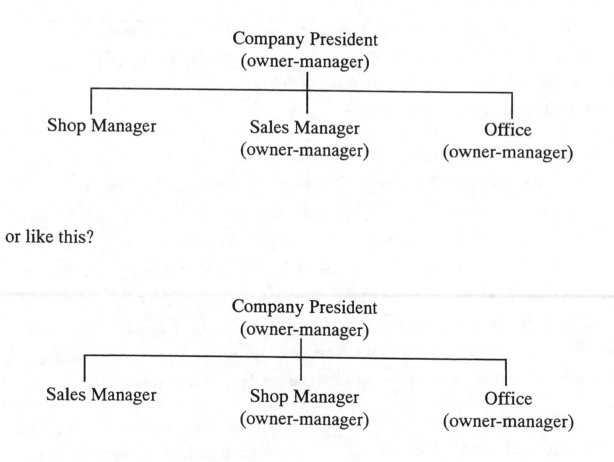

or like this?

As the service business grows, its organization chart could look like this:

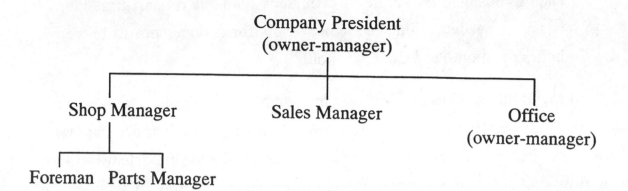

The Financial Plan

Clearly the most critical section of your business plan document is the financial plan. In formulating this part of the planning document, you will establish vital schedules that will guide the financial health of your business through the troubled waters of the first year and beyond.

Before going into the details of building the financial plan, it is important to realize that some basic knowledge of accounting is essential to the productive management of your business. If you are like most business owners, you probably have a deep and abiding interest in the product or services that you sell or intend to sell. You like to do what you do, and it is even more fulfilling that you are making money doing it. There is nothing wrong with that. Your conviction that what you are doing or making is worthwhile is vitally important to success. Nonetheless, the income of a coach who takes the greatest pride in producing a winning team will largely depend on someone keeping score of the wins and losses.

The business owner is no different. Your product or service may improve the condition of mankind for generations to come, but, unless you have access to an unlimited bankroll, you will fail if you don't make a profit. If you don't know what's going on in your business, you are not in a very good position to assure its profitability.

Most Convenience Food Store businesses will use the "cash" method of accounting with a system of record keeping that may be little more than a carefully annotated checkbook in which is recorded all receipts and all expenditures, backed up by a few forms of original entry (invoices, receipts, cash tickets). For a Sole Partnership, the business form assumed by this Management Aid, the very minimum of recorded information is that required to accurately complete the Federal Internal Revenue Service Form 1040, Schedule C. Other business types (partnerships, joint ventures, corporations) have similar requirements but use different tax forms.

If your business is, or will be, larger than just a small supplement to family income, you will need something more sophisticated. Stationery stores can provide you with several packaged small business account systems complete with simple journals and ledgers and detailed instructions in understandable language.

Should you feel that your accounting knowledge is so rudimentary that you will need professional assistance to establish your accounting system, the classified section of your telephone directory can lead you to a number of small business services that offer a complete range of accounting services. You can buy as much as you need, from a simple "pegboard" system all the way to computerized accounting, tax return service and monthly profitability consultation. Rates are reasonable for the services rendered and an investigative consultation will usually be free. Look under the heading, "Business Consultants," and make some calls.

Let's start by looking at the makeup of the financial plan for the business.

The Financial plan includes the following:

1. Financial Planning Assumptions - these are short statements of the conditions under which you plan to operate.

- Market health
- Date of start-up
- Sales build-up ($)
- Gross profit margin
- Equipment, furniture and fixtures required
- Payroll and other key expenses that will impact the financial plan

2. Operations Plan - Profit and Loss Projection - this is prepared for the first year's Budget. Appendix A-11.

3. Source of Funds Schedule - this shows the source(s) of your funds to capitalize the business and how they will be distributed among your fixed assets and working capital.

4. Pro Forma Balance Sheet - "Pro forma" refers to the fact that the balance sheet is before the fact, not actual. This form displays Assets, Liabilities and Equity of the business. This will indicate how much Investment will be required by the business and how much of it will be used as Working Capital in its operation.

5. Cash Flow Projection - this will forecast the flow of cash into and out of your business through the year. It helps you plan for staged purchasing, high volume months and slow periods.

Creating the Profit and Loss Projection.

Appendix A-11. Create a wide sheet of analysis paper with a three inch wide column at the extreme left and thirteen narrow columns across the page. Write at the top of the first page the planned name of your business. On the second line of the heading, write "Profit and Loss Projection." On the third line, write "First Year."

Then, note the headings on Appendix A-11 and copy them onto your 12-column sheet, copy the headings from the similar area on Exhibit A. Then follow the example set by Appendix A-11 and list all of the other components of your income, cost and expense structure. You may add or delete specific loans of expense to suit your business plan. Guard against consolidating too many types of expenses under one account lest you lose control of the components. At the same time, don't try to break down expenses so discretely that accounting becomes a nuisance instead of a management tool. Once again, Exhibit A provides ample detail for most businesses.

Now, in the small column just to the left of the first monthly column, you will want to note which of the items in the left-hand column are to be estimated on a monthly (M) or yearly (Y) basis. Items such as Sales, Cost of Sales and Variable expenses will be estimated monthly based on planned volume and seasonal or other estimated fluctuations. Fixed Expenses can usually be estimated on a yearly basis and divided by twelve to arrive at even monthly values. The "M" and "Y" designations will be used later to distinguish between variable and fixed expense.

Depreciation allowances for Fixed Assets such as production equipment, office furniture and machines, vehicles, etc. will be calculated from the Source of Funds Schedule.

Appendix A-11 describes line by line how the values on the Profit and Loss Projection are developed. Use this as your guide.

Source of Funds Schedule

To create this schedule, you will need to create a list of all the Assets that you intend to use in your business, how much investment each will require and the source of funds to capitalize them. A sample of such a list is shown below:

Asset	Cost	Source of Funds
Cash	$2,500	Personal savings
Accounts Receivable	3,000	From profits
Inventory	2,000	Vendor credit
Pickup truck	5,000	Currently owned
Packaging machine	10,000	Installment purchase
Office desk and chair	300	Currently owned
Calculator	75	Personal cash
Electric typewriter*	500	Personal savings

*   A note about office equipment, test use or rent two or more brands that appear to meet your needs and select the one with which you feel most comfortable. Don't be afraid to ask others who have had to make this decision for advice. Compatibility of your system with those of potential typesetting services or printers should be of high considerations. If you are not quite sure, consider renting or leasing the equipment until you are. Service contracts on such complex electronic gear are usually a good insurance policy.

Before you leave your Source of Funds Schedule, indicate the number of months (years x 12) of useful life for depreciable fixed assets. (An example, the pickup truck, the packaging machine and the furniture and office equipment would be depreciable.) Generally, any individual item of equipment, furniture, fixtures, vehicles, etc., costing over $100 should be depreciated. For more information on allowances for depreciation, you can get free publications and assistance from your local Internal Revenue Service office. Divided the cost of each fixed asset item by the number or months over which it will be depreciated. You will need this data to enter as monthly depreciation on your Profit and Loss Projection. All of the data on the Source of Funds Schedule will be needed to create the Balance Sheet.

Creating the Pro Forma Balance Sheet

Appendix A-13. This is the Balance Sheet Form. There are a number of variations of this form and you may find it prudent to ask your banker for the form that the bank uses for small business. It will make it easier for them to evaluate the health of your business. Use this to get started and transfer the data to your preferred form later. Accompanying Appendix A-12 which describes line by line how to develop the Balance Sheet.

Even though you may plan to stage the purchase of some assets through the year, for the purpose of this pro forma Balance Sheet, assume that all assets will be provided at the start-up.

Cash Flow Projection

An important subsidiary schedule to your financial plan is a monthly Cash Flow Projection. Prudent business management practice is to keep no more cash in the business than is needed to operate it and to protect it from catastrophe. In most small businesses, the problem is rarely one of having too much cash. A Cash Flow Projection is made to advise management of the amount of cash that is going to be absorbed by the operation of the business and compares it against the amount that will be available.

SBA has created an excellent form for this purpose and it is shown as Appendix B. Your projection should be prepared on 13-column analysis paper to allow for a twelve-month projection. Appendix B represents a line by line description and explanation of the components of the Cash Flow Projection which provides a step-by-step method of preparation.

Resources

U.S. Small Business Administration
Office of Business Development

Business Development Publication
MP15

Convenience Food Store
Business Associations for the Entrepreneur

National Association of Convenience Stores (NACS)
1605 King St.
Alexandria, VA 22314-2792
Kerley Leboeuf, Pres.
PH: (703) 684-3600   FX: (703) 836-4564
Founded: 1961   Members: 2,400

**National Advisory Group, Convenience Stores/Petroleum Markets Association
(NAG)**
2063 Oak St.
Jacksonville, FL 32204-4492
Hugh K. Howton, Pres.
PH: (904) 384-1010   FX: (904) 387-3362
Founded: 1983   Members: 500

Notes

Chapter 7

Managing The Business

Delegating work, responsibility, and authority is difficult in a small business because it means letting others make decisions which involved spending the owner/manager's money. At a minimum, he should delegate enough authority to get the work done, to allow assistants to take initiative, and to keep the operation moving in his absence. Coaching those who carry responsibility and authority in self-improvement is essential and emphasis in allowing competent assistants to perform in their own style rather than insisting that things be done exactly as the owner/manager would personally do them is important. "Let others take care of the details" is the meaning of delegating work and responsibility. In theory, the same principles for getting work done through other people apply whether you have 25 employees and one top assistant or 150 to 200 employees and several keymen yet, putting the principles into practice is often difficult.

Delegation is perhaps the hardest job owner/managers have to learn. Some never do. They insist on handling many details and work themselves into early graves. Others pay lip service to the idea but actually run a one-man shop. They give their assistants many responsibilities but little or no authority. Authority is the fuel that makes the machine go when you delegate word and responsibility. If an owner/manager is to run a successful company, he must delegate authority properly. How much authority is proper depends on your situation. At a minimum, you should delegate enough authority: (1) to get the work done, (2) to allow keymen to take initiative, (3) to keep things going in your absence.

The person who fills a key management spot in the organization must either be a manager or be capable of becoming one. A manager's chief job is to plan, direct, and coordinate the work of others. He should possess the three "I's" — Initiative, Interest, and Imagination. The manager of a department must have enough self-drive to start and keep things moving. Personality traits must be considered. A keyman should be strong-willed enough to overcome opposition when necessary.

When you manage through others, it is essential that you keep control. You do it by holding a subordinate responsible for his actions and checking the results of those actions. In controlling your assistants, try to strike a balance. You should not get into a keyman's operations so closely that you are "in his hair" nor should you be so far removed that you lose control of things.

You need feedback to keep yourself informed. Reports provide a way to get the right kind of feedback at the right time. This can be daily, weekly, or monthly depending on how soon you need the information. Each department head can report his progress, or lack of it, in the unit of production that is appropriate for his activity; for example, items packed in the shipping room, sales per territory, hours of work per employee.

For the owner/manager, delegation does not end with good control. It involves coaching as well, because management ability is not required automatically. You have to teach it. Just as important, you have to keep your managers informed just as you would be if you were doing their jobs.

Part of your job is to see that they get the facts they need for making their decisions. You should be certain that you convey your thinking when you coach your assistants. Sometimes words can be inconsistent with thoughts. Ask questions to make sure that the listener understands your meaning. In other words, delegation can only be effective when you have good communications.

Sometimes an owner/manager finds himself involved in many operational details even though he does everything that is necessary for delegation of responsibility. In spite of defining authority, delegation, keeping control, and coaching, he is still burdened with detailed work. Usually, he had failed to do one vital thing. He has refused to stand back and let the wheels turn.

If the owner/manager is to make delegation work, he must allow his subordinates freedom to do things their way. He and the company are in trouble if he tries to measure his assistants by whether they do a particular task exactly as he would do it. They should be judged by their results — not their methods. No two persons react exactly the same in every situation. Be prepared to see some action taken differently from the way in which you would do it even though your policies are well defined. Of course, if an assistant strays too far from policy, you need to bring him back in line. You cannot afford second-guessing.

You should also keep in mind that when an owner/manager second-guesses his assistants, he risks destroying their self-confidence. If the assistant does not run his department to your satisfaction and if his shortcomings cannot be overcome, then replace him. But when results prove his effectiveness, it is good practice to avoid picking at each move he makes.

Notes _____

Chapter 8

Business Resource Information

Books

Steps To: Small Business Start-up,
  by Linda Pinson and Jerry Jinnett (Kaplan Publishing, 2006).

Blue's Clues for Success: The 8 Secrets Behind a Phenomenal Business,
  by Diane Tracy (Dearborn, 2001).

Entrepreneur Magazine's Start Your Own Business, 3rd. ed.,
  by Rieva Lesonsky (Entrepreneur Press, 2004).

MBA in a Day: What You Would Learn at the Top-Tier Business Schools,
  by Steven Stralser (New York: John Wiley & Sons, 2004).

Own Your Own Corporation: Why the Rich Own Their Own Companies and Everyone Else Works for them,
  by Garrett Sutton, Robert T. Kiyosaki, and Ann Blackman (Warner Books, 2001).

Portratis of Success: 9 Keys to Sustaining Value in Any Business,
  by James Olan Hutcheson (Dearborn, 2002).

Small Time Operator: How to Start Your Own Business, Keep Your Books, Pay Your Taxes, and Stay Out of Trouble, (Small Time Operator, 27th Edition)
  by Bernard B. Kamoroff, (Bell Springs Publishing, 2005).

Successful Business Planning in 30 Days: A Step-by-Step Guide for Writing a Business Plan and Starting Your Own Business,
  by Peter J. Patsula (Patsul Media, 2000).

Straight Talk About Starting and Growing Your Business,
  by Sanjyot P. Dunung (McGraw Hill, 2006).

Associations and Organizations

U.S. Department of Commerce
14th Street and Constitution Avenue NW
Room 5055
Washington, DC 20210
Phone: 202-482-5061
Web site: *rvwm.mbda.gov*

U.S. Department of Labor
200 Constitution Avenue NW
Washington, DC 20210
Web site: *www.dol.gov*

Federal Trade Commission
600 Pennsylvania Avenue NW
Washington, DC 20580
General information: 202-326-2222
Anti-trust and competition issues: 202-326-3300
Web site: *www.ftc.gov*

U.S. Small Business Administration (SBA)
403 3rd Street SW
Washington, DC 20416
Phone: 202-205-7701
Web site: *www.sba.gov*

SBA Regional Offices
- Region 1, Boston: 617-565-8415
- Region 2, New York: 212-264-1450
- Region 3, King of Prussia, PA: 215-962-3700
- Region 4, Atlanta: 404-347-995
- Region 5, Chicago: 310-353-5000
- Region 6, Ft. Worth, TX: 817-885-6581
- Region 7, Kansas City, MO: 816-374-6380
- Region 8, Denver: 303-844-0500
- Region 9, San Francisco: 415-744-2118
- Region 10, Seattle: 206-553-7310

Internal Revenue Service
Washington, DC 20224
Phone: 800429-1040
Web site: *www.irs.ustres.gov*

The IRS has an expansive Web site where you can find a great deal of tax help and a state-by-state guide for locating state tax information. There are also numerous tax publications (all numbered) including:

- Tax Guide for Small Business, Publication #334
- Self-Employment Tax, Publication #533
- Business Expenses, Publication #535

For tax forms go to *www.irs.ustres.gov/forms*

International Franchise Association
1350 New York Avenue NW
Suite 900
Washington, DC 20005-4709
Phone: 202-628-8000

American Association of Franchises and Dealers
P.O. Box 81887
San Diego, CA 92138-1887
Phone: 800-733-9858
Web site: *www.aafd.org*

Associations and Organizations

**National Association of Women
  Business Owners**
1411 K Street NW
Suite 1300
Washington, DC 20005
Phone: 202-347-8686
Fax: 202-347-4130
Information service line: 800-556-2926
Web site: *www.nawbo.org*

The National Association for the Self-Employed
1023 15 Street NW
Suite 1200
Washington, DC 20005-2600
Phone: 202-466-2100
Web site: *www.nase.com*
The NASE works to help the self-employed
make their businesses successful and provides
numerous benefits and services. It was formed
over twenty years ago by small business owners.

**Occupational Safety and Health Administra-
tion (OSHA)**
200 Constitution Avenue NW
Washington, DC 20210
Web site: *www.osha-slc.gov*

Institute For Occupational Safety and Health
Phone: 800-35-NIOSH or 513-533-8328
Web site: *www.cdc.gov/niosh*

Dun & Bradstreet
Austin, Texas 78731
Phone: 800-234-3867
Web site: *www.dnb.com*
For over 160 years, D&B has been providing
companies with information and assistance in
making key business decisions.

**American Entrepreneurs for
  Economic Growth**
1655 North Fort Myer Drive
Suite 850
Arlington, VA 22209
Phone: 703-524-3743
Web site: *www.aeeg.org*

**National Association of
  Home-Based Businesses**
10451 Mill Run Circle
Suite 400
Owings Mills, MD 21117
Phone: 410-363-3698
Web site: *www.usahomebusiness.com*

U.S. Census Bureau
Washington DC 20233
Phone: 301-457-4608
Web site: *www.census.gov*

U.S. Patent and Trademark Office
General Information Services Division
Crystal Plaza 3, Room 2CO2
Washington, DC 20231
Phone: 800-786-9199 or 703-308-4357
Web site: *www.uspto.gov*

U.S. Securities & Exchange Commission
450 Fifth Street NW
Washington, DC 20549
Office of Investor Education
  and Assistance: 202-942-7040
Web site: *www.sec.gov*

Associations and Organizations

**American Association of
  Home Based Businesses**
Fax: 301-963-7042
P.O. Box 10023
Rockville, MD 20849
Website: *www.aahbb.org*

American Small Businesses Association
800-942-2722
8773 IL Route 75E
Rock City, IL 61070

Home Business Institute
561-865-0865
P.O. Box 480215
Delray Beach, FL 33448
Website: *www.hbiweb.com*

Marketing Research Association
860-257-4008
1344 Silas Deane Highway, Suite 306,
Rocky Hill, CT 06067
Website: *www.mra-net.org*

**National Association of the
  Self-Employed (NASE)**
800-252-NASE (800-232-6273)
P.O. Box 612067
DFW Airport
Dallas, TX 75261-2067
Website: *www.nase.org*

Magazines

Entrepreneur Magazine, Business Start-Ups Magazine, and **Entrepreneur's Home Office Entrepreneur Media, Inc.**
2392 Morse Avenue
Irvine, CA 92614
Phone: 714-261-2325
Web site: *www.entrepreneurmag.com*

Forbes
60 Fifth Avenue
New York, NY 10011
Phone: 212-620-2200
Web site: *www.forbes.com*

Inc. Magazine
38 Commercial Wharf
Boston, MA 02110
Phone: 617-248-8000 or 800-2340999
Web site: *www.inc.com*

My Business Magazine
Hammock Publishing, Inc.
3322 West End Avenue
Suite 700
Nashville, TN 37203
Phone: 615-385-9745

Consumer Goods Manufacturer
Edgell Communications
10 West Hanover Avenue
Suite 107
Randolph, NJ 07869

Minority Business Entrepreneur
3528 Torrance Boulevard
Suite 101
Torrance, CA 90503
Phone: 310-540-9398
Web site: *www.mbemag.com*

Workforce ACC Communications
245 Fischer Avenue
Suite B-2
Costa Mesa, CA 92626
Phone: 714-751-4106
Web site: *www.workforceonline.com*

Websites

www.allbusiness.com
A comprehensive site with resources for small and medium sized businesses.

www.bizweb.com
A guide to some 47,000 companies.

www.bplan.com
Numerous sample business plans for various industries.

www.bspage.com
The Business Start page includes a short course on starting a business, tips, and reviews of top business books.

www.business.gov
The U.S. Business Advisor is a one-stop shop for working with the many government agencies that impact upon business.

www.businessfinance. com
A major online source for finding potential investors.

www.businessnation.com
Business news, a library, discussions, opportunities, and resources.

www.businesstown.com
Information and articles from starting to selling your business.

www.catalogconsultancy.com
Information and guidance for catalog and direct mail businesses.

www.chamber-of-commerce.com
Links to local chamber of commerce Web sites, and e-mail addresses.

www.financenet.com
Sponsored by the US Chief Financial Officers Council, FinanceNet has a wealth of information and resources available specializing in public financial management.

www.globalbizdirectory.com
Massive director of retail, agricultural, mining, and numerous other business-related organizations and associations. Includes a state-by-state and international listing database.

www.gomez.com
Gomez offers business new and detailed report cards and consumer responses on e-commerce Web sites in various sectors.

www.homebusiness.com
Detailed information and business solutions for the home base business.

www.hoovers.com
Provides detailed business and company information, industry report links, professional help, business news, and more.

www.ideacafe.com
A good place for news, tips, expert advice ideas, and schmoozing with other small business owners.

www.inc.com
A wealth of articles and advice about starting and growing your business from the folks at Inc. Magazine.

www.marketingsource.com/associations
Find any association in any industry at this valuable resource site.

www.morebusiness.com
Articles, tips, sample business and marketing plans, legal forms contracts, a newsletter, and more offered for entrepreneurs.

www.nasbic.org
The National Association of Small Business Investment Companies promotes growth in the business sector through numerous programs.

Library Resources

**Almanac of Business and
Industrial Financial Ratios**
(Prentice-Hall). Provides ratios and industry
norms in actual dollar figures derived from IRS
data. Each industry includes performance
indicators such as total assets, cost of
operations, wages, and profit margins.

**American Wholesaler and
Distributor Directory**
(Gale Research). Provides listings of
wholesalers and distributors sorted by product
category and state.

Catalog of Catalogs
(Woodbine House). Contains descriptions and
contact information for more than 14,000
catalogs, indexed by subject and company name.

Directory of Manufacturers' Sales Agencies
(Manufacturing Agents National Association).
Lists manufacturers' sales agencies
alphabetically and by state. Also has information
on how to select a sales agent.

Encyclopedia of Associations
(Gale Research). Guise to national and
international associations; contains contact
information and descriptions; indexed by name,
key word, and geographic area.

Financial Studies of the Small Business
(Financial Research Associates). Organized by
industry; contains financial ratios and indicators
for small and microbusinesses.

Lifestyle Market Analyst
(Standard Rate & Data Service). Reference book
containing demographic and psychographic
statistics for metropolitan statistical areas in the
United States.

Small business Profiles
(Gale Research). Contains sources of
information related to starting specific types of
small businesses. Typical entries include start-up
information, trade associations and publications,
statistics, and supply sources.

Thomas Food Industry Register.
Directory of food manufacturers and suppliers to
the food industry.

Thomas Register of Manufacturing.
Directory of most manufacturing firms; includes
company profile and contact information.

The Small Business Administration

The U.S. Small Business Administration was established in 1953 to provide financial, technical, and management assistance to entrepreneurs. Statistics show that most small business failures are due to poor management. For this reason, the SBA places special emphasis on business management training that covers such topics as planning, finance, organization, and marketing. Often, training is held in cooperation with educational institutions, chambers of commerce, and trade associations. Prebusiness workshops are held on a regular basis for prospective business owners. Other training programs are conducted that focus on special needs such as rural development and international trade. One-on-one counseling is provided through the Service Corps of Retired Executives (SCORE) and Small Business Development Centers (SBDC). The SBA strives to match the needs of a specific business with the expertise available.

To access the SBA: Online http://www.sba.gov
                               SBA Answer Desk 800-827-5722

SCORE is a volunteer program that helps small business owners solve their operating problems through free one-on-one counseling and through a well-developed system of low-cost workshops and training sessions. To located a SCORE counseling center in your area or to consult online, access the following site: http://www.score.org
SBDCs are generally located or headquartered in academic institutions and provide individual counseling and practical training for prospective and current business owners. To locate a center near you, log on to http://www.sba.gov/sbdc.

A Concise Guide To Starting Your Own Business

Page A-2

Guide Overview

A concise overview of the complete guide to starting and operating a successful business.

The following topics are presented:

- Business Plan for Small Businesses.
- Getting Started
- Deciding Where To Start The Business
- Business Patronage Statistics
- Site Location
- Site Selection Criteria — Some General Questions.
- Choosing The Proper Method of Organization
- What Is A Corporation?
- Estimating Start-up Costs
- Preparing An Income Statement
- Preparing A Balance Sheet
- Marketing The Business
- Marketing Planning — An Outline for Marketing
- Advertising Media
- Management and Getting The Work Done
- Sample Organization Chart
- Summary of the Business Plan
- Guide Summary
- Reference Materials

Business Plan for Small Businesses

Page A-4

Getting Started

Following is a list of what you need to accomplish to insure that your business endeavor will head in the right direction.

1. Define your educational background and work experience

2. Survey all basic types of businesses.

3. Define what type of business matches your experience and educational background.

4. Choose only the business that you would like to own and operate.

5. Define what products or services your business will be marketing.

6. Define who will be using your products/services.

7. Define why they will be purchasing your products/ services.

8. List all competitors in your marketing area.

Deciding Where to Start the Business

Will your business fulfill a need in the area you plan to bring your business to? This section provides you with some important information you need to examine before taking your ideas any further:

1. Decide where you want to live.

2. Choose several areas that would match your priorities.

3. Use the list that follows as a guide to see if your location will match the estimated population needed to support your business. The numbers which follow the type of business indicate the typical number of inhabitants per year.

Business Patronage Statistics

Food Stores
Grocery Stores 1,534
Meat and Fish
(Sea Food) Markets . . . 17,876
Candy, Nut, and
Confectionery Stores . . 31,409
Retail Bakeries 12,563
Dairy Products Stores . . . 41,587

Eating and Drinking
Restaurant, Lunch Rooms . 1,583
Cafeterias 19,341
Refreshment Places 3,622
Drinking Places 2,414

General Merchandise
Variety Stores 10,373
General Merchandise 9,837

Apparel/Accessories Stores
Women's Ready-To-
Wear Stores 7,102
Women's Accessory and
Specialty Stores 25,824
Men's and Boy's Clothing
and Furnishings 11,832
Family Clothing 16,890
Shoe Stores 9,350

Furniture, Home Furnishings, and Equipment Stores
Furniture Stores 7,210
Floor Covering 29,543
Drapery, Curtains, and
Upholstery Stores 62,585
House, Appliances 12,485
Radios and TV's 20,346
Record Shops 112,144
Musical Instruments 46,332

Building Materials, Hardware, and Farm Equipment Dealers
Lumber and other Building
Materials Dealers 8,124
Paint, Glass, and Wallpaper
Stores 22,454
Hardware Stores 10,206
Farm Equipment Dealers . 14,793

Automotive Dealers
Motor Vehicle Dealers,
New and Used Cars 6,000
Motor Vehicle Dealers,
Used Cars only 17,160
Tire, battery, and
Accessory Dealers 8,800

Boat Dealers 61,500

Household Trailer Dealers . 44,746

Gasoline Service Stations . . . 1,395

Miscellaneous
Antique and Secondhand
Stores 17,170
Book and Stationery Stores 28,580
Drugstores 4,268
Florists 13,531
Fuel Oil Dealers 25,000
Garden Supply Stores . . . 65,000
Gift, Novelty Shops 26,000
Hobby, Toy, and Game
Shops 61,000
Jewelry Stores 13,400
Optical Goods Stores 62,800
Sporting Goods Store 27,000

From *Starting and Managing a Small Business of Your Own, 1973;*
Small Business Administration, Washington, DC

Page A-6

Site Location

1. Define your number of inhabitants per store.

2. Locate several sites/locations that will match your inhabitants per stores.

3. Define population and its growth potential.

4. Define local ordinances and zoning regulations that you will need in order to start your type of business.

5. Define your trading area and all competitors in your trading area.

6. Define parking need, for your kind of business.

7. Define special needs, etc., lighting, heating, ventilation.

8. Define rental cost of site/location.

9. Define why customers will come to your site/location.

10. Define the future of your site/location as to population growth.

11. Define your space needs and match with site/location selection.

12. Define the image of your business and make sure it matches your site/location.

Site Selection Criteria — Some General Questions

- Is the site centrally located to reach my market?

- What is the transportation availability and what are the rates?

- What provisions for future expansion can I make:

- What is the topography of the site (slope and foundation)?

- What is the housing availability for workers and managers?

- What environmental factors (schools, cultural, community atmosphere) might affect my business and my employees?

- What will the quality of this site be in 5 years, 10 years, 25 years?

- What is my estimate of this site in relation to my major competitor?

- What other media are available for advertising? How many radio and television stations are there?

- Is the Quantity and quality of available labor concentrated in a given area in the city or town? If so, is commuting a way of living in that city or town?

- Is the city centrally located to my suppliers?

- What are the labor conditions, including such things as relationships with the business community and average wages and salaries paid?

- Is the local business climate healthy, or are business failures especially high in the area?

- What about tax requirements? Is there a city business tax? Income tax? What is the property tax rate? Is there a personal property tax? Are there other special taxes?

- Is the available police and fire protection adequate?

- Is the city or town basically well planned and managed in terms of such items as electric power, sewage, and paved streets and sidewalks?

Page A-8

Choosing the Proper Method of Organization

Listed below are legal forms of business available to the small business entrepreneur:

Sole Proprietorship

Advantages
- Simple to start
- All profits to owner
- Owner in direct control
- Easy entry and exit
- Taxed as individual

Disadvantages
- Unlimited liability
- "Jack-of-all-trades"
- Capital requirement limited
- Limited life
- Employee turn-over

Partnership

Advantages
- Easy to originate
- Credit rating
- Talent combination
- Legal Contract

Disadvantages
- Unlimited liability
- Misunderstandings
- Partner withdrawal
- Regulations

Corporation

Advantages
- Limited liability
- Expansion potential
- Transfer of ownership
- Retain employees

Disadvantages
- Double taxation
- Charter restrictions
- Employee motivation
- Legal regulations

What Is A Corporation?

A corporation is an artificial being, invisible, intangible, and existing only in contemplation of the law," wrote Chief Justice John Marshall. In other words, the corporation exists as a separate entity apart from its owners, the shareholders. It makes contracts; it is liable; it pays taxes. It is a "legal person".

The corporation is the most complex of the three major forms of business ownership. The corporation stands as a separate legal entity in the eyes of the law. The life of the corporation is independent of the owners' lives. Because the owners, called shareholders, are legally separate from the corporation, they can sell their interests in the business without affecting the continuation of the business. When a corporation is founded, it accepts the regulations and restrictions placed on it by the state in which it is incorporated and any other state in which it chooses to do business. Generally, the corporation must report its financial operations to the state's attorney general on an annual basis.

Estimating Start-up Costs

Item	Amount
Fixtures and Equipment	$ _____
Building & Land (If Needed)	_____
Store and/or Office Supplies	_____
Remodeling and Decorating	_____
Deposits on Utilities	_____
Insurance	_____
Installation of Fixtures	_____
Legal Fees	_____
Professional Fees	_____
Telephone	_____
Rental	_____
Salaries and Wages	_____
Inventory if Retailing	_____
Licenses and Permits	_____
Advertising and Promotion	_____
TOTAL Estimated Start-up Cost	$_____

Preparing An Income Statement

What is an Income Statement?

The income statement shows the income received and the expenses incurred over a period of time. Income received (sales) comes essentially from the sales of the merchandise or service which your business is formed to sell. Expenses incurred are the expired costs that have been incurred during the same period of time.

Plan A Budgeted Income Statement For One Year

1. Project Total Sales
2. Estimate Total Expenditures
3. Example Listed Below for Income Statement

Percents	1	2	3	4	5	6	7	8	9	10	11	12
Sales												
Cost of Sales												
Gross Profit												
Expenditure												
Rent Expense												
Supplies												
Wages/Salaries												
Utilities												
Insurance												
Depreciation												
Interest												
Miscellaneous												
Net Profit												

Preparing A Balance Sheet

What is a Balance Sheet?

The balance sheet shows the assets, liabilities and owner's net worth in a business as of a given date.

- Assets are the things owned by your business, including both physical things and claims against others.
- Liabilities are the amounts owned to others, the creditors of the firm.
- Net worth or owner's equity is the owner's claim to the assets after liabilities are accounted for.

A Budgeted Balance Sheet For One Year

- List all your business property at their cost to you: these are your assets.
- List all debts, or what your business owes on all your property; these are your liabilities.
- Take your total property balance (Assets), and subtract the total amount you owe (Liabilities).
- The balance is what you own in your business called (Owner's equity).
- Add Total Liabilities (2) & Total Owner's Equity (3).
- Listed on the next page is an example of a balance sheet.

NAME OF BUSINESS
BALANCE SHEET
DATE

ASSETS

Current Assets
  Cash
  Accounts Receivable   _____
Merchandise Inventories   _____
    TOTAL CURRENT ASSETS   _____

Fixed Assets
  Land
  Building   _____
  Equipment   _____
    TOTAL FIXED ASSETS   _____
        TOTAL ASSETS   1). _____

LIABILITIES

Current Liabilities
  Accounts Payable   _____
  Note Payable   _____
  Payroll Taxes Payable   _____
    TOTAL CURRENT LIABILITIES   _____

Long-term Liabilities
  Mortgage Payable   _____
  Long-term Note   _____
    TOTAL LONG-TERM LIABILITIES   _____
        TOTAL LIABILITIES   2). _____

OWNER'S EQUITY

Proprietor's Capital   3). _____

    TOTAL LIABILITIES & OWNER'S EQUITY   (2 &3). _____

Marketing The Business

1. Define Your Market
   - Type of Customers
   - Age, Income, Occupation of your customers
   - Type of Trading Area

2. Promotion of Your Business
   - Advertising
   - Setting your Image

3. Customer Policy Plan
   - Develop a Customer Profile
   - Customer Services
   - Customer Needs

4. Pricing Your Products/Services
   - Know all your Costs
   - Know your Profit Margin
   - Know Competitor's Price
   - Know what Return you want on your Investment

5. Sales Promotion
   - Coupons
   - Contests
   - Displays
   - Demonstrations
   - Giveaways
   - Banners

6. Public Relations
   - Newspaper Article
   - Contact Trade Association
   - Radio Promotion
   - TV Promotion

7. Segmentation of your Market
   - Age
   - Occupation
   - Income
   - Location
   - Education
   - Hobbies

Marketing Planning

Outline for Marketing

I.   Product/Service Concept:
   a. Name of product or service
   b. Descriptive characteristics of product or service
   c. Unit sales
   d. Analysis of market trends

II. Number of Customers in your Market Area:
   a. Profile of customers
   b. Average customer expenditure
   c. Total market

III. Your Market Potential:
   a. Total market divided by competition
   b. Total market multiplied by percent who will buy your product

IV. Needs of Customers:
   a. Identification
   b. Pleasure
   c. Social approval
   d. Personal interest
   e. Price

V.   Direct Marketing Sources:
   a. Trade magazines
   b. Trade associations
   c. Small Business Administration (SBA)
   d. Government Publications
   e. Yellow pages
   f. Marketing directories

VI   Customer Profile:
   a. Geographical
   b. Gender
   c. Age range
   d. Income brackets
   e. Occupation
   f. Educational level

Advertising Media

Medium	Market Coverage	Type of Audience
Daily newspaper	Single community or entire metro area: zoned editions sometimes available	General
Weekly newspaper	Single Community	Residents
Telephone Directory	Geographical area or occupational field served by the directory	Active shoppers for goods or services
Direct mail audience	Controlled by the advertiser	Controlled
Radio audience	Definable market area	Selected
Television audience	Definable market area surrounding TV Stations	Various
Outdoor	Entire metro area	General auto drivers
Magazine	Entire metro area or magazine region	Selected audience

Management and Getting the Work Done

1. Define your objective for starting your business.

2. Define your goals: profit growth for first three years.

3. Develop an organization chart of your business.

4. Define your personal needs.
   - Hiring proper employees
   - Training employees
   - Motivation

5. Define all responsibility for each person in your business.

6. Define all authority.
   - Who will hire and fire?
   - Who will select and train all personnel?
   - Who will keep the important records as to inventory, purchasing, sales records, cash records, etc.?

7. Define all laws and regulations that will be requirements for operating your business.

8. Review all duties and tasks with all your employees.

9. Write a summary of all the important tasks that you want to finish in your first year in business.

Sample Organization Chart

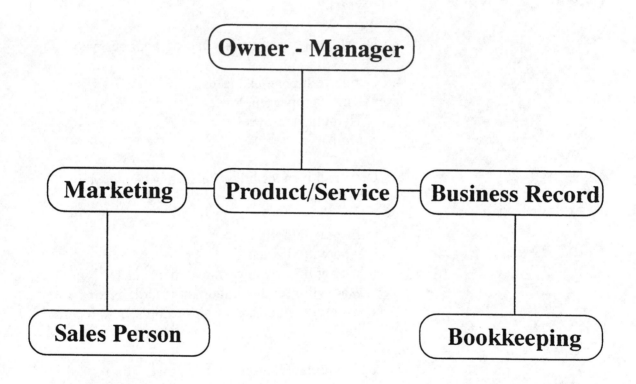

Summary of The Business Plan

Name of Business
BUSINESS PLAN
Date

1. Define your business
   * Name all principals
   * Address and phone number

2. Define your products or services

3. Define your market

4. Define your site or location

5. Advertising Plan
   * Budget
   * Media

6. Chart of Start-up cost

7. Worksheet of Income Statement
   * Revenue/Income
   * Expenses

8. Worksheet of Balance Sheet
   * Assets (Property)
   * Capital (Owner's Equity)
   * Liabilities (Debts)

9. Personnel Outline
   * Number of Employees
   * Staffing & Training

10. Management Organization
    * Organization Chart
    * Evaluation Policy
    * Job Profile

11. Special Statement
    * 3-Year Sales Schedule
    * Cash Flow
    * 3-Year Expense Schedule

Appendix A Summary

1. Contact your State Commerce Department for guidelines in starting your business.

2. Contact your City/County Clerk for guidelines in starting your business.

3. Contact all other Governmental Centers that will furnish you all the legal regulations and tax laws that will effect your business.
   - State Government
   - Internal Revenue Service
   - State Employment Security Commission
   - Department of Treasury
   - City Governmental Units

     a. Fire
     b. Police
     c. Zoning
     d. Building Permits
     e. Health
     f. Water & Sewage

4. Township Government
   - Local Legal Requirements
   - Local Taxes
   - Local Health Permits
   - Local Zoning Laws

**Reference
Materials**

Management Aids Titles

Contact the.

**Small Business Administration
P.O. Box 15434
Fort Worth, TX 76119**

for the following booklets:

* Number 2.025   Thinking About Going Into Business
* Number 2.010   Planning and Goal Setting For Business
* Number 1.016   Sound Cash Management
* Number 1.001   The A.B.C's. of Borrowing
* Number 1.008   Break-even Analysis
* Number 2.022   Business Plan For Service Firms
* Number 2.023   Business Plans for Retail Firms

Notes _____

Appendix B

HOUSEHOLD NEEDS

Many small business start-ups fail due to their inability to support their owners. Rarely do new businesses support their owners from the start. However, many individuals fail to recognize this fact. In addition, then, to a sound business plan, it is necessary for an owner to project the household cash needs month-by-month for the first three years of the business' operation. As a new business owner, you should be able to support yourself until your new business is able to support you in a manner to which you are accustomed.

MONTHLY HOUSEHOLD CASH NEEDS

Regular NON-BUSINESS Income
Spouse's salary _____
Investment income _____
Social security _____
Other income _____
Retirement benefits _____
Less taxes _____
Net monthly income _____

Regular Monthly Expenses

Housing
    Mortgage/Rent _____
    Utilities _____
    Homeowner's insurance _____
    Property taxes _____
    Home repairs _____

Living Expenses
    Groceries _____
    Telephone _____
    Tuition _____
    Transportation _____
    Meals _____
    Child care _____
    Medical expenses _____
    Clothing _____
    Personal _____

Insurance Premiums
    Life insurance _____
    Disability insurance _____
    Auto insurance _____
    Medical insurance _____

Debt Repayment
    Auto loans _____
    Consumer debt _____

Discretionary Expenses
    Entertainment _____
    Vacation _____
    Gifts _____
    Retirement contributions _____
    Investment savings _____
    Charitable contributions _____
    Dues, magazines, etc. _____
    Professional fees _____
    Other _____

Total Monthly Expenses _____

Monthly Surplus/Deficit _____

Total Year Surplus/Deficit _____
(Monthly x 12)

Available Assets to Cover Deficit
    Checking accounts _____
    Savings accounts _____
    Money market accounts _____
    Personal credit lines _____
    Marketable securities _____
    Lump-sum retirement/
      severance _____
    Other assets _____

Total Assets _____

NEEDED RESERVES
    Total Assets-Deficit _____

PERSONAL FINANCIAL STATEMENT

This is a picture of your personal financial condition to date. It is a very important part of any loan application and/or interview, especially when a loan for a projected new business is under consideration.

PERSONAL FINANCIAL STATEMENT

_____ _____ , 19 _____

Assets
Cash
Savings accounts
Stocks, bonds, other securities
Accounts/Notes receivable
Life insurance cash value
Rebates/Refunds
Autos/Other vehicles
Real estate
Vested pension plan/Retirement accounts
Other assets

TOTAL ASSETS $ _____

Liabilities

Accounts payable
Contracts payable
Notes payable
Taxes
Real estate loans
Other liabilities

TOTAL LIABILITIES $ _____

TOTAL ASSETS $ _____

LESS TOTAL LIABILITIES $ _____

NET WORTH $ _____

BALANCE SHEET

A balance sheet is a current financial statement. It is a dollars and cents description of your business (existing or projected) which lists all of its assets and liabilities.

BALANCE SHEET

_____ _____ , 19 _____

	YEAR 1	YEAR II
Current Assets		
Cash		
Accounts receivable		
Inventory		
Fixed Assets		
Real estate		
Fixtures and equipment		
Vehicles		
Other Assets		
License		
Goodwill		
TOTAL ASSETS	$_____	$_____
Current Liabilities		
Notes payable (due within 1 year)	$_____	$_____
Accounts payable		
Accrued expenses		
Taxes owed		
Long-Term Liabilities		
Notes payable (due after 1 year)		
Other		
TOTAL LIABILITIES	$_____	$_____
NETWORTH (ASSETS minus LIABILITIES)	$_____	$_____

TOTAL LIABILITIES plus NET WORTH should equal ASSETS

PROFIT AND LOSS STATEMENT

A profit and loss statement is a detailed earnings statement for the previous full year (if you are already in business). Existing businesses are also required to show a profit and loss statement for the current period to the date of the balance sheet.

PROJECTED PROFIT AND LOSS STATEMENT

	Month 1	Month 2	Month 3	Month 4	Month 5	Month 6	Month 7	Month 8	Month 9	Month 10	Month 11	Month 12
Total Net Sales												
Cost of Sales												
GROSS PROFIT												
Controllable Expenses												
Salaries												
Payroll taxes												
Security												
Advertising												
Automobile												
Dues and subscriptions												
Legal and accounting												
Office supplies												
Telephone												
Utilities												
Miscellaneous												
Total Controllable Expenses												
Fixed Expenses Depreciation												
Insurance												
Rent												
Taxes and licenses												
Loan payments												
Total Fixed Expenses												
TOTAL EXPENSES												
NET PROFIT (LOSS) **(before taxes)**												

CASH FLOW PROJECTIONS

A cash flow projection is a forcast of the cash (checks or money orders) a business anticipates receiving and disbursing during the course of a month. Well managed, the cash flow should be sufficient to meet the cash requirements for the following month.

CASH FLOW PROJECTIONS

	Start-up or prior to loan	Month 1	Month 2	Month 3	Month 4	Month 5	Month 6	Month 7	Month 8	Month 9	Month 10	Month 11	Month 12	TOTAL
Cash (beginning of month														
Cash on hand														
Cash in bank														
Cash in investments														
Total Cash														
Income (during month)														
Cash sales														
Credit sales payment														
Investment income														
Loans														
Other cash income														
Total Income														
TOTAL CASH AND INCOME														
Expenses (during month														
Inventory or new material														
Wages (including owner's)														
Taxes														
Equipment expense														
Overhead														
Selling expense														
Transportation														
Loan repayment														
Other cash expenses														
TOTAL EXPENSES														
CASH FLOW EXCESS (end of month)														
CASH FLOW CUMULATIVE (Monthly)														

Getting Down to Business...

Convenience Food Store

An Instructional Guide for Creating A Small Business
by Jerre G. Lewis, M.A.
& Leslie D. Renn, M.S.

Convenience Food Store

Convenience food stores are under constant pressure to change according to consumer needs and preference, and examination of them as a small business venture should take this into account. The advent of self-service in the early 1950's started a trend toward greater selection and greater selection and greater variety with resulting larger stores. The need for smaller, more convenience type stores, where fast service was the main advantage, became evident. Prices of merchandise at these convenience stores were generally higher than their larger competitors, but to many consumers the stores were attractive for limited shopping that saved time and also provided longer hours of operation.

Costs of constructing, equipping and opening new convenience food stores are rising as the bidding becomes more competitive for prime sites. Today to open a typical 2400 square foot convenience store, will require an investment of at least 575,000. A 32,000 square foot supermarket being built in a suburban location will require a capital investment of at least $800,000. Medium stores range in between the two. The retail food industry has traditionally shown a low profit margin. A recent survey of 84 participating retailers, operating 320 stores, showed the average pretax income for all stores to be 2.1 percent of sales. This pretax income varied from a low of 1.3 percent for stores with weekly sales of $40,000-$50,000 to a high of 2.5 percent for stores with weekly sales of $60,000-$70,000. Even though 10 to 20 percent is usually a store's average gross profit, the various major departments in food stores, such as meat, produce, and grocery, vary widely from the store average. A full-time grocery store will usually have about 70 percent of its sales in grocery items; 20 to 25 percent in meat and 6 percent in produce. Many convenience stores do not handle fresh produce or meat, but do carry a deli counter or foreign food items.

The high cost of wages is a big concern for all stores. Labor cost in a full line grocery usually runs from 8 percent to 11 percent of sales and account for one-half of the expenses. A store with marginal sales would have a tremendous wage cost. The rise in minimum wage has caused many stores to cut out their entry-wage labor, such as the carry out people. Theft, a cause of 1 percent to 3 percent loss of sales, is also a major concern of store managers. There are three types of theft: Employee; shoplifting; and vendor. Of these three, employee theft is the most prevalent. Management must set up strong regulations to cope with this problem.

Convenience stores are subject to local, state and federal regulations, and particular attention must be paid to sanitation matters. Wage and hour laws must be complied with, as well as regulations of Occupational Safety and Health Administration (OSHA). Opportunities exist for enterprising individuals to own their own convenience stores such as through franchising with supervisory assistance for operators which can often be secured with a capital investment of $10,000 to $20,000. Today, as well as in-the future. An owner operator of a convenience food store needs the entrepreneur's ambition to be the boss without the security of a guaranteed salary, but the willingness to accept the risks and responsibilities of an owner. Industry training programs will enhance education and help keep the owner operator abreast of new industry trends and developments. The store of today will probably not be what the customer wants and expects a few years from now. The store owner will need to anticipate trends and tare advantage of them.

Four things involved in planning to open a convenience food store are: Deciding what products, customers, competition, and problems your store might have: Deciding what personal qualities and skills you will need: Knowing how to compete well; and learning about the legal requirements for running the business. Your customers will be anyone who likes the kinds of food and products your store carries. Once you have decided what type of store to open, you must advertise and bring your customers in. A small convenience food store cannot serve everyone. Your success will depend on choosing a particular type of customer and then selling products they prefer.

There usually is some kind of competition to consider. When you open a convenience food store, you will be competing with other stores that carry the same products (even though they may not be as good as yours). Supermarket and grocery chains may carry the same or similar foods and at a discount price since they deal in larger quantities. In the convenience food store business, a unique product or a distinctive image will give you a competitive edge. It helps to have a catchy name that will help people remember your store.

You don't have to be an expert in the line of business that you are thinking of going into, but you do have to be willing to learn. And there are basic qualities which you must have -or be wilting to develop—if you are going to start any business. The most important quality is the ability to organize your mind and your life. In running a small business like a convenience food store, you will deal with many different people, keep schedules, meet deadlines, organize paperwork, pay bills, etc. These are part of every business. It is also important to be able to read carefully. You will have to keep many written records, and you will have to fill out a lot of government forms. As a business owner, you can't be afraid of numbers either. The math involved is mostly simple arithmetic—addition, subtraction, and some multiplication—but you must be good at it for your business to succeed. You must also: Like people and enjoy working with them; be reasonable and non judgmental in dealing with people; have patience with your customers and staff, and with the problems of waiting for a small business to grow; and be willing to work very hard.

All these qualities are important for any small business owner. A knowledge of nutrition, food storage, and preparation methods is helpful for a convenience food store owner too. But the real secret to success is building personal relations with customers. Customers appreciate a friendly, low-key approach and an owner who knows them by name. These are the customers who will come back to your store again and again.

There are several things you can do to compete well: Do research before starting the business to help you decide where to locate and which items you want to offer; try to be unique. Offer products and items that other stores do not offer; keep the quality of your products and your service high; establish an image that is professional, yet friendly. When you are small, you can offer more personalized service than the larger stores. Legal requirements vary according to the types of products you sell and where you are located. To find out what licenses you will need, contact the department of consumer affairs, the small business administration, or a trade association of wholesale and retail grocers. Here is a list of permits and licenses that may be required: A seller permit (also called a sales tax permit); an Employer Identification (EI) number from the Internal Revenue Service (IRS); a business license from the city hall or the county government center; and a fictitious trade name registered with the city or county government if the name of your store is not your name.

Convenience food stores will have to conform to local zoning laws, building codes, health requirements, and fire and police regulations. If you pay salaries you must meet requirements for payroll deductions and have necessary employee insurance such as worker's compensation and liability coverage. You will need fire insurance, crime coverage, automobile insurance (for company-owned cars), and business interruption insurance. Convenience food stores are risky businesses to get into. Make sure you have the right personality and know enough about the business before you get into it. Your competition may be tough. A convenience food store that offers quality and personalized service can succeed if you have the patience and energy for the work.

Once you have decided to open a convenience food store, you must decide where to locate and what services and products to offer. Before you choose a location for your store, you will need to do some homework. First, think about the area where you will open your store. Pick the area that gives you the best chance for success. Study the area and consider the following; the neighborhood's potential for growth; the characteristics of the residents (income, ages, interests, and occupations); the number of similar stores in the area; and the type of neighborhood—residential, commercial, industrial, rural or urban.

Perhaps you are thinking about moving out of the city to set up a convenience food store in the country. A large percentage of these rural shops fail. Rural areas often do not believe enough people who want and can afford convenience food store items. Your choice of location will be one of the most important decisions you make, so consider it carefully. Many people would like to locate in their own neighborhood, but is it a good business area? How many people shop in your neighborhood? Is there enough parking? Are there already similar businesses in the area? Look for a location where a service gap exists. For example, look for an area with many businesses and offices and a shortage of convenience food stores. Before you rent a storefront, find out why it's vacant. Talk to nearby shopkeepers and learn as much as you can about the area and it's shoppers. Be careful if there are several empty buildings for rent in the area. Besides being a sign of a poor business area, empty buildings make poor neighbors—shoppers tend to stay away from them. A heavy flow of walking traffic passing by or close to the door is a sign of a good place to locate. Look the store over carefully. Is the building right for you? Is it large enough, or is it perhaps too large? Will it need a lot of remodeling? Can you afford it? What kind of rental agreement will you have to sign? Be sure to have the building examined by the local building inspector and if you plan to prepare or serve food on the premises, by the health inspector. You do not want to learn after you have moved in that you must spend a considerable amount of money bringing the plumbing up to code. In choosing your location, be alert for these trouble signs. Avoid: Areas with a large number of existing and successful competitors; sites where the insurance rates will be very high -such as next to old buildings; and sites that are difficult for people to get to. You can do your own informal market research. A professional real estate agent can also help you choose a location for your convenience food store.

Community banks, newspapers, census information, chamber of commerce and utility company reports, and city and county planning councils all provide information on the area and the specific site you choose for your store. This advance work will help you choose the best site to locate your store. Rent is a major expense for convenience food stores. When you start looking at store sites, you should consider the amount of rent you can afford to pay. Rent may be very high in a downtown area or an established shopping center. Shopping centers sometimes add area maintenance fees to the monthly rent. An out-of-the-way location may be less expensive, but will your customers be able to get to your store? Will you have to pay more for advertising in order to make your store known? Rent is normally paid in one of two ways: Flat rental rate, which calls for a set monthly amount; or percentage of sales agreement, in which you agree to pay a base amount and/or a percentage of the monthly sales. The percentage of sales agreement is often used by shopping centers. Some landlords will also include an escalator clause in their rent agreements. This clause allows the landlord to raise the rent over a period of time. Rental agreements are usually very complex. For example, a rental agreement from a shopping center may run from 40 to 60 pages. It would be wise to have your lawyer and an insurance agent review the agreement before you sign. All new businesses need money to get started. Your own savings and loans from family or friends will likely be the main source for your new business. However, you may also have to borrow some of your starting capital from a bank, loan office, or government agency. Lenders will want to know a lot about you and your business plan before they will lend you money. You will have to show that you are a good business risk. You will be asked to provide the following information: Personal background information (a resume'); description of your business (the business plan); and a statement of financial need. When you ask for a loan, the lender will want to know what kind of store you want to start and how you plan to run it. The lender will be looking at how carefully you have planned your business. This is the time for you to think carefully about what you want to do. Your business plan should be clearly and simply written. You should include the following information: The kind (and name) of store you want to open; the items you will sell and the services you will provide; the area and site of your business, and why you chose it; the target customers (the market) you want to attract; your competition in the area; your management plan and strategy for success; and the number and type of employees you plan to hire.

How much you will need depends on the type of business you are starting and the type of person you are. If you are willing to work hard, to make a few sacrifices, to live on canned beans for a while, you can start a successful business for relatively little money. Loans are hard to get… banks are less willing than ever to take chances on new and untested businesses, and on new and untested business owners. But the doors are not completely closed. Banks still make business loans, and a bank might just make one to you. Banks will generally lend up to 50 percent of the money you need to start your business if they can be convinced that your business has a good chance to succeed, that you are competent and reliable, and that you have a good plan for running your business. To open a convenience food store you may need to put down a fairly large amount of money. This money will cover start-up costs, machinery, remodeling fees, beginning inventory, and three months' operating and personal costs. You may consider either buying or renting equipment and furniture for your store. Renting equipment may help keep start up costs low, but renting may be more expensive in the long run.

Owning and running a convenience food store involves many responsibilities, including hiring and being in charge of staff. If you manage your employees well, they can help build your business by: Selling skillfully to your customers; doing the work efficiently and on time; and providing products and services that are of the highest quality. In hiring new employees, you will have to screen applicants carefully. You will want to hire responsible and reliable people. The image and reputation of your store depends on your doing this job well.

When you screen people for a job, have them: Fill out a detailed job application; come in for a personal interview; and give you a list of personal references. First, make a list of the qualities and attitudes you are looking for in your employees. Hiring decisions begin with a detailed description of the job to be filled. Make sure the applicant gets a copy of this job description—it tells what is expected. You may want to use part-time help to keep your costs down. If you are aware of customer shopping patterns, you can schedule your employees effectively. More people may be needed at certain times, such as during lunch hours, holidays, and sales. However, there may be training—in sales, operating the machines, bookkeeping tasks, or whatever responsibilities your employee will have. Employee salaries will be a large expense in operating your convenience food store. To attract top-notch help, the salary you offer must be competitive or slightly better than similar stores in your area. Employees should also be offered some kind of health insurance and retirement plan. Let your employees know you are concerned about their job satisfaction. Some stores give their employees discounts on items they buy there for themselves.

Give your staff enough training and instruction to allow them to carry out their jobs. In addition, give them written information on your store policies so that everyone will know what you expect of them. Include such things as employment requirements (health and insurance coverage), work assignments and how they are made, dress code, fringe benefits, working hours, and overtime compensation. Then, when everyone knows the rules and regulations, follow them in a businesslike way. Keeping the people you hire and the customers you serve happy involves establishing good relations and contributes to the positive reputation of your store.

Careful selection of the best goods from reliable suppliers is a key concern for convenience food store owners. Some suppliers may specialize in one whole line of items, like dairy products. Other suppliers handle the full line of merchandise your store will carry. Your choice of suppliers will depend on the merchandise, products, and services you plan to emphasize in your store, the quality of inventory you want to maintain, and the extra services the supplier offers.

Here are some basic points to keep in mind when buying merchandise for your convenience food store: Buy what you know will sell in your store. Each convenience food store sells to different customers with different needs. What will sell in one store may not sell in another; include a variety of items on your shelves. Store owners know that customers can get tired of the same old stuff. To fight this boredom and to add a little variety to your store, add different or unusual merchandise; buy what you like, but keep your customers in mind. A convenience food store owner may be tempted to buy the items and food he or she likes. But the customer's tastes must come first; be flexible. You will have to keep an open mind about your store's inventory. When you buy supplies, you might see an item you haven't noticed before that would appeal to your customers; don't overbuy. Sometimes suppliers have sales on certain merchandise. You might be tempted to load up on these items. Remember, however, that what you can't sell ends up sitting on the shelf; buy in depth. Don't buy a little of this and a little of that. Your store may end up looking like a junk store. Pick a few products, and stock them in fairly large quantities. Buying in depth tells your customers: This is what we believe in. Smart buying involves buying the right merchandise for your customers: In the right quantity (not overstocking); of the right quality; at the best prices; and from reliable suppliers who will give you the best service and prompt delivery. Most convenience food stores will have accounts with a number of suppliers. When you start looking for suppliers, there are four basic considerations: When merchandise is to be shipped, how much time you have before you pay the bill, and the discount you will be given for paying in cash.

Some suppliers offer 8/10 EOM (end-of-month) terms. This means that stores that pay within ten days after the end of the month may subtract 8% from the bill. But if your payment is late, you will owe the full amount at the end of that month. For example, if you pay a bill dated October 5 by November 10, you can take an 8% discount. If you wait until next month, you will have to pay the full amount. You will often have to arrange for delivery of the merchandise from the supplier's warehouse to your store. Studying shipping methods and rates will let you choose a delivery method that is economical and will get the goods to you on time. You may consider trucks, the postal service, united parcel service, railway or air express. Your choice will depend on cost, distance, how fast you need the merchandise, and the size of your order.

Many convenience food stores handle perishable items—foods that need to be refrigerated. For example, if you sell cheese and other dairy products, fast delivery in refrigerated trucks will be important. If you need nonperishables, immediate deliver, is not essential.

Delivery time varies depending on the type of merchandise, shipping point, and delivery method. Some deliveries will take only a few days. Others, especially imported items, may take weeks or months. You will have to plan your buying schedule carefully.

The number of suppliers you buy from should be small. Suppliers favor their more loyal customers, especially if they know you personally. They may give you better delivery time and buying terms. They will be more helpful if, for any reason, you want to return an order. They will also give you tips on special deals and industry news.

Good management of your store's inventory is essential to keep you foods and produce fresh and to give your customers what they want. There are several reasons why you should have some kind of inventory control system: To keep track of the foods, merchandise, and supplies that go into and out of your store; to help you plan for future orders; to give you an idea of the dollar value of your inventory; and to let you know which foods, products, and merchandise are popular and which ones do not sell.

Your best bet is to keep your inventory control system simple. Personal observation is one way of keeping track of stock. By arranging your inventory, you can tell by looking what has been sold and what needs to be re-ordered. You can take occasional physical inventory counts to get a precise number of items sold, or unsold. This should be done on a regular basis. Last, there is the book method (perpetual inventory). This is a way of estimating the stock on hand by using this formula: Current inventory = inventory at beginning of period + owner purchases made during period - sales during period.

Store owners must keep accurate records of their purchases and sales. Purchase order forms and inventory cards will help you. Pricing is basically a matter of striking a balance. You want to set your prices high enough that your costs are covered and low enough that you can stay in line with your competition. In setting your prices, there are four main things to consider: The cost of goods sold (the amount of money you spend on the goods you sell the customers); your operating expenses; the amount of profit you want to make on your sales; and your competition (the going prices—and what people are willing to pay).

Stock turnover is the number of times a store's inventory is sold and replaced during the year. You will want to have a healthy flow of goods in and out of your store. Frequent stock turnover is one sign of a successful store operation. Most stores try to sell their merchandise as fast as they can. This way, perishable goods are not lost because of spoilage. The stores will also have ready cash to buy more merchandise and products and to improve their inventory.

Turnover rates will be different, depending on the types of food and merchandise your store carries. A low turnover rate may tell you that too much money is tied up in slow-moving merchandise. If your perishable items are unsold, you will have to throw them out and lose money. When you have a low rate of turnover, you should take a close look at both your products and your prices.

A basic step in making a profit is selling goods for more than they cost you. You but your supplies and inventory from your suppliers at wholesale prices. The difference between the wholesale cost of the merchandise and the price you charge your customers (the retail price) is called mark-up.

The selling price you set on items should cover wholesale costs, transportation costs, and operating expenses. Operating expenses may include: Rent payment for the store; salaries of employees; advertising and promotion costs; utilities, insurance fees, and taxes; and costs of operating, maintaining, and repairing any necessary machinery or equipment.

Your prices must be competitive. There is usually a going rate to be considered—the average price your competitors charge for the products. Take the time to find out your competition's prices. Keep these in mind when you set your own prices. Customers will not be happy paying higher prices unless you also offer extra services. These services may include free delivery, gift wrapping, or extra help from salespeople. Wines may improve with age, but other products may get moldy and stale. Greenish cheese, for example, will not sell. If your merchandise is not selling, you may consider marking it down for a quick sale before it spoils. If you hold on to slow-moving stock, you may end up having to throw it out and take a loss on your investment. Many stores may have two to four big sales each year. There are many different kinds of sales such as grand opening sales, holiday sales, and end-of-season sales. Some items may be priced very low in order to attract customers to the store. There are many other reasons to lower the prices of goods in your store. You may charge less if you decide you don't want your business to expand at a fast rate. If you like things the way they are and a large profit is not absolutely essential for you, you may lower your prices.

Prices may go down if operating expenses go down, or if you can figure out an especially efficient way of operating your store. Prices may go down if your wholesale costs are reduced and you can afford to pass these savings on to your customers. If you are planning to raise prices, you might want to ask for more money now than you think you currently need. If the state of the economy is such that expenses are constantly going up, adding more to the price now will mean you won't have to raise prices again soon (and upset your customers a second time).

You can ask higher prices if your store is unique—if you are the only convenience food store of your kind in the area. You can ask for more if you provide special services—

for example, delivery services. This is because you will probably have to put in more time and effort in order to get the job done. You can ask for more if your wholesale costs and your operating expenses go up for example, as the price of gasoline goes up, so will your costs to deliver your goods: As the price of wheat goes up, so will the price of flour. You can ask for more if you need to hire more employees to assist you in your business or if you want to improve one aspect of your business. For example, you may wish to replace your old refrigerator with a newer efficient (and more expensive) refrigerator. Every business needs customers. Advertising is a good way of getting the word out and telling shoppers about your store, special events, services, and prices. The purpose of advertising is to attract customers. It is a way of telling people what you can do for them. What are the best ways to advertise your store? Take a good look at yourself and your customers. Ask yourself these questions: What business an I in? How is my store different from my competition? What quality merchandise do I sell.? What kind of store image do I want to advertise? What customer services do I offer? Who are my customers? What are their tastes? What do they buy from me? A good advertising campaign can be very expensive, but you can substitute imagination and good public relations for money. The first thing to do is to find out what your customers read and listen to. Then plan your advertisingm, here are ways you can advertise your store. Although direct mail is expensive, it: Reaches a selected audience (your target customers); is effective for special uses such as a mail order business, announcing new products and/or services, welcoming new customers, announcing special events and sales; and offers a great variety of formats (catalogs, letters, fliers, coupons, brochures). Newspapers are the most commonly used form of advertising, prices of ads will vary depending on the newspaper's circulation and the size of your ad. Although newspaper ads have relatively short life spans, they: Are relatively inexpensive for the large number of people they reach; are easily and quickly changed and can be placed in a particular newspaper or sections of a paper to reach a select audience; and are available in various formats — as classified ads, inserts to regular editions, and special shoppers' guides.

The cost of local radio and television ads can be expensive. But radio and television ads can be very effective for telling people about sales and other special store events.

Public relations includes the image you develop for your store and all your dealings with the public. It is simply the way people feel about your store-the thing that makes people think of you when a friend asks them where to buy something. Two excellent business-getters for your store are (a) its appearance from the outside and (b) word-ofmount advertising. These two public relations methods will probably bring in more customers than all your other advertising methods combined.

In addition, directories such as the yellow pages are very important in advertising your store. This is usually the first place people look when they are trying to find a particular product. Directories: Have long life spans; will list your store and/or product alphabetically so potential customers can easily locate your ad; and are easily available to the public.

These are only a few of the ways stores tell the public about themselves. In addition, you may consider transit advertising on buses or trains and specialty advertising such as food and cooking shows, calendars, t-shirts, balloons, buttons, and matches. You can also design a distinctive logo that can be printed on shopping bags and fliers.

Qualities Of A Good Ad

Here are some tips you can use when you begin to plan your ads: A good ad should be simple, informative, and truthful; make sure your ads are easy to recognize. Give your ads a consistent personality and style. Use a distinctive store logo; show the benefit to the reader of shopping at your store. Customers want to know "what's in it for me?"; Feature the "right" item. Show merchandise that is timely, wanted, in stock, and typical of your store. Specify brand merchandise whenever possible; state a price or range of prices. If prices are low, tell people why—because of sales or special offers; include the store name, address, telephone number, and hours.

Ads that call for prompt action are very effective. Put action in your words. Use terms your reader will understand. Get right to the point. Make every word count. You may want to include discount coupons. Mentioning limited quantities or a short time period for a special sale will also encourage people to act quickly

Find out the costs of advertising before you decide what type of ad you want to use. In one sense, your decision on how much to spend for advertising will come down to: How little can I spend and still do the job that needs to be done? Don't skimp too much, however. Remember that advertising is an "investment" you must make to bring in sales.

Keeping Financial Records

Keeping financial records is a must for any business. Good records will help you keep track of your income and expenses, spot problems, and file financial statements and tax returns. In this unit you will learn how to keep track of your money from sales on a day-to-day basis and how to fill out a daily cash sheet.

Cash Sales

Cash sales are usually recorded when customers pay for their purchases at the time of the sales. The salesperson fills out a sales slip. Cash sales are then rung up on a cash register. Sales slip receipts and cash register tapes form the basis of any bookkeeping system. This information will tell you the total amount of sales for that day.

When a customer buys something, he or she is given a receipt. Receipt provides the customer with proof of payment. This proof is necessary in case the customer wants to return the purchase. A second copy of the sales slip is kept at the store. This is one way to keep track of store inventory.

To keep your business running smoothly, you will need answers to questions such as these: How many sales were made during the day? What types of merchandise were sold and how many of each? What was the dollar amount of the sales? Did the customer take advantage of any of the special services? What credit terms were given to the customer?

Keeping Track Of Credit Sales

Most convenience food store are retail stores. This means that their business comes mainly from their "over-the-counter" sales to private individuals. Accepting credit cards will eliminate most of the headaches of keeping track of credit accounts. You will not

---

No: 1123

SALES SLIP

DATE   6/18
CUSTOMER   Joanna Howard
ADDRESS   123 Main St.

Description of Sale	Price
1 doz. plain bagels	2.55
1 pkg. cream cheese	.27
1 pkg. hot dogs	1.23

Cash   __X__.   Subtotal   4.05
Charge   _____   Sales Tax   .26
                                      TOTAL $4.31

need credit books, and you will never have to hound people to pay their bills. The credit card companies will handle all the paper work and will guarantee payment of the bill whether or not the customer has paid them. They will also charge a fee for this service. But for most businesses, the fee is worth the savings in effort, paperwork, and aggravation.

Credit cards are a popular way of buying. The advantage of accepting credit cards are that: (1) it makes buying easy and convenient for the customer: (2) it reduces the risk of your giving credit and not getting paid: And (3) your money is not tied up in debts and unpaid bills.

When you accept credit cards, you should follow these steps (1) check the expiration date on the card and refuse to accept expired cards: (2) have the customer sign the sales receipt and compare the signature to the one on the credit card: And (3) telephone for approval on sales over a certain amount (usually $50 or $100).

Easy come and easy go: The daily cash sheet

A daily cash sheet can be used to keep track of the money coming in and going out of your business each day. All income information, taken from each day's sales and credit receipts and cash register tapes, should be added up and recorded on this form. Sales may be recorded by the type of item sold. The sales are recorded on the left side of the form and are added up daily. On the right side you are to enter the money you paid out each day—the money you spent on inventory and your operating expenses.

At the end of each month, or at the end of the year, these daily figures are added up to show your income and expenses. It will also show you the days and the months that are slow and busy so that you can better plan for your buying, advertising, promotional sales, etc. Good daily records will help you fill out an income statement (also known as a profit? Loss statement). The next unit covers profit? loss statements.

Keeping your business successful

Every small business owner wants to be successful. This is obvious. But how to be successful is not always as obvious.

There are three important ways to keep your business successful: Make sure you have enough cash: Keep your profits up and costs down: And improve or change your business practices when necessary.

In the last unit you learned how to keep track of your cash flow on a daily basis. This same system can be used on a monthly or yearly basis. In this unit you will also learn ways to change your business to increase sales and show more profit.

Keeping track of profits

Profit is a reward for your hard work. Net profit is defined as the amount of money left over from your sales (revenues) after all your business expenses have been paid (net profit= gross profit - expenses). Keeping careful records of your sales and expenses is a necessary step in figuring out your profits. When you add all the figures over the whole year, you will come up with a profit/loss (P/l) statement. A profit/loss statement will tell you what your business has taken in and spent and how much profit you have made over the year. Yearly p/l statements will tell you the direction your business is taking from year to year.

How to calculate a profit/loss statement

A profit/loss statement consists of five main parts: (1) revenues: The money coming into your store from cash and credit sales; (2) cost of goods sold: The inventory you start with at the beginning of the year plus purchased during the year minus the amount of inventory on hand at year end; (3) gross profit: The amount of money brought in minus the cost of good sold: (4) expenses: The money you spent on operating expenses for your store. This includes employees' salaries, rent, utilities, supplies, advertising, etc.; (5) net profit: The amount of money left over from your gross profit after all the store's expenses have been paid or gross profit minus expenses.

Profit/Loss Statement

		Year 1	Year 2
Revenues			
Cash Sales		$ 74,000	$ 92,000
Credit Sales		$ 31,000	$ 60,000
	TOTAL	$ 105,000	$ 152,000
Cost of Goods Sold		$ 42,000	$ 60,800
Gross profit		$ 63,000	$ 91,200
Expenses			
Salaries		$ 24,000	$ 29,000
Building Expenses		$ 6,000	$ 9,840
Supplies		$ 2,150	$ 3,000
Advertising		$ 1,000	$ 2,000
Utilities		$ 10,000	$ 16,000
Insurance		$ 2,000	$ 4,000
	TOTAL	$ 45,150	$ 63,840
NET PROFIT		$ 17,850	$ 27,360

Profit and Loss Ratios

Profit and expense ratios can be used to help you compare your stock's performance over a few years. The information on your p/l statement is used to calculate the profit ratio and the expense ratio of your store. You can use the following formulas to compute these ratios:

$$\text{Profit ratio} = \frac{\text{Net Profit}}{\text{Revenues}}$$

$$\text{Expense Ratio} = \frac{\text{Expenses}}{\text{Revenues}}$$

If we compute the profit and expense ratios for the years 1 and 2 they look like this:

Year 1	Year 2
$\text{Profit Ratio} = \dfrac{17,850}{105,000} = 17\%$	$\text{Profit Ratio} = \dfrac{27,360}{152,000} = 18\%$
$\text{Expense Ratio} = \dfrac{45,150}{105,000} = 43\%$	$\text{Expense Ratio} = \dfrac{63,840}{152,000} = 42\%$

What do these figures mean? As you can see, in year 2 they earned more profit dollars and had a slightly higher profit ratio than in year 1.

By year 2 the word had gotten around about the business, and more people were buying their product. Even though the costs of inventory (cost of goods sold had increased, sales have also increased. By this time the costs of salaries, rent, and all other expenses had also increased. But they had not increased as fast as revenues. Therefore, in year 2 a larger percentage of revenues was going into the store's profit than into expenses as compared to year 1.

Improving profits

If you feel your profits are too low, or that your store is not growing quickly enough, you can try to improve your business. There are three basic ways to increase profits in any business: (1) increase sales; (2) raise prices; or (3) reduce expenses.

Profits and sales may be low for any number of reasons. You must try to find out why your sales are down before you decide what to do. There are two ways to go about increasing sales in order to raise your profits: (1) improve the visibility of your store (more advertising?: (2) change your image and the merchandise you sell.

More advertising is an increased expense. But this is an example of spending money in order to make more money. You may consider changing the image of your store and developing a new theme. Your inventory will reflect your new store image.

Expanding your business

Many people find that the best way to increase their sales is to offer new services. Find out what else your customers want: Then figure out what you can do and if you can afford to do it. For example, adding new and more convenient services for your customers (like a new stock 'in a different location or a deli service in your present store) is one way to bring in customers and expand your business.

Time does not stand still: Neither do your competitors or the tastes and demands of the customers you serve. Unless you stay on your toes, you may find yourself with an empty store and no customers. But you should remember that if you expand your store, you will also be increasing your workload. You will have to consider hiring more employees. And the larger your store grows, the less you will be able to supervise all the details.

You should make the decisions to expand your store very carefully by taking a close look at how much you like the convenience food store business, what type of image and personality you want for your store, and what your future plans are.

Summary

You can calculate your store's profits and compare them year-to-year by recording income and expenses on a profit/loss statement. If you want to increase profits you must increase sales, raise prices, or reduce your operating costs.

Today, more than ever, price-conscious customers are buying carefully and holding back on spending until they find the right item at the right price. But an efficient and imaginative store owner who is in touch with customer tastes can be successful in the convenience food store business. By maintaining a distinctive store image, a reputation for quality, and a concern for customer satisfaction, a small convenience food store can always attract shoppers who are looking for "something special" to buy.

Appendix D

INSURANCE CHECKLIST

TYPE OF INSURANCE	PURCHASE	DO NOT PURCHASE
PROPERTY INSURANCE:		
Fire	_____	_____
Windstorm	_____	_____
Hail	_____	_____
Smoke	_____	_____
Explosion	_____	_____
Vandalism	_____	_____
Water Damage	_____	_____
Glass	_____	_____
LIABILITY INSURANCE	_____	_____
WORKERS' COMPENSATION	_____	_____
BUSINESS INTERRUPTION	_____	_____
DISHONESTY:		
Fidelity	_____	_____
Robbery	_____	_____
Burglary	_____	_____
Comprehensive	_____	_____
PERSONAL:		
Health	_____	_____
Life	_____	_____
Key Personnel	_____	_____

Special Appendix

Web Site Marketing

Business Web Site
an
Effective Marketing Tool

More than 100 million people use the Internet each day. A website offers help in marketing your small business. Your web site can help level the playing field for small businesses who compete with big businesses. It can enable small business to expand their business nationally or internationally.

What makes a good web site?

A good web site shows by doing; it proves rather than states. Instead of making claims, it provides evidence.

Evidence can take several forms:

- Case Studies showing how your efforts solved a previous client's problems.

- Testimonials from satisfied clients.

- Reprints of articles you've written or reviews of your work.

Education, however, remains the best way to establish credibility. To the extent prospects leave your web site better informed about your product or service, the easier it is to gain their respect (and their purchase order).

Three steps to creating your own business web site.

Today's tools make web publishing accessible to small businesses without programming experience. For example, Microsoft® Publisher 97 includes PageWizard design assistants, web deign elements and design checkers to help your build a workable web site.

Step one:

Choose a structure and a look. Your site should be structured and designed to best tell your story. But where do you start? Using the Page Wizard, you can choose from pre-designed options that can later be customized so that establishing a structure and "look" is easy.

Step two:

Tell your story. Next, simply select the sample headlines and text provided and replace them with words that describe what you have to offer.

Step three:

Check your work and post your site. The design in Publisher 97 goes through your web site element by element, identifying potential problems. Then, the web publishing wizard guides you through the process of posting your web site on the local Internet service provider or on-line service of your choice.

Remember, with millions of web sites, you may have to market your web site as well as your small business to get traffic for your business. The web site can be an inexpensive way of effectively building your small business.

10 tips for Web Site Online Marketing

1. Put up a simple web page.
2. Use a name that will attract people
3. Give away advice and information
4. Have lots of e-mail correspondence
5. Provide customized pages for users.
6. Visit user groups
7. Get on mailing lists
8. Arrange links with related sites
9. Make sure you're in every possible directory
10. Do not "SPAM"

The principals of a Website

In today's business world, a good website is essential to any advertising campaign, but you need to understand, that all websites are not created equal. Nearly any web development company can build you a site that looks good, but if the public cannot locate it, does it really exist?

First off you need to understand that websites are only limited by your imagination, but again I stress, no matter how creative, how interactive, or how great it looks, if the public cannot easily find it, what good is it? Each search engine has created a list of criteria that your site must comply with, in order to be placed in the top 10 listings; this criteria list varies from search engine to search engine and is not made public.

Optimization; The first three rules of any business also applies to websites; location, location, location. 85% of all internet users use the search engines to find what they are looking for.

Nearly 85% of all searches performed in the world go through Google, Yahoo, and MSN, with AOL at a distant 4th with about 8%. This means that the thousands of other search engines share the last 7 to 10%. Less than 3% of the public will search past the 3rd page, therefore it is imperative for your website to work, it must have top rankings!

The 10 second rule; the average internet user will search through 7 sites before finding what they are looking for. Once your site is located, you have approximately 10 seconds to entice the visitor to go deeper into your site. To accomplish this, your home page needs to provide a brief summary of your site. The visitor must be able to scan this page and conclude that your site contains the information they are seeking within that 10 second window. You can always test the success of your home page by checking your web stats and comparing the visitors to pages viewed. If the average is 2 pages per visitor or better, than you know the average visitor likes what they see.

Contact Info; Studies have shown that the average internet user would rather contact you by telephone than by email whenever possible, yet many websites do not contain a phone number or it is buried in the contact us page. A good website will make the contact information available on every page. If your site is intended to be fully automated, then at least display a "take an action" link prominently on each page.

Newsletters; Electronic newsletters are greatly overlooked. A good monthly newsletter will keep your business at the front of their thoughts. Always be sure the newsletter contains a quick link to your website.

As I previously stated, any web company can make a site look good, but only a few websites have the potential to work, to actually tell your story and bring in business.

Although you can buy a website development program, and possibly build your own site, the odds are greatly stacked against you. Less than one thousandth of one percent of the websites out there can be easily located. Another important tip is to hire a company that not only specializes in regional or global optimization (depending upon your market area), but a company that offers an all inclusive annual program with options for future years at a guaranteed renewal price. I have provided the following link to Sutherland's Web Services, (www.sws.tc). SWS, is a good example of an all inclusive, web development firm that specializes in regional optimization. The all inclusive services of Sutherland's includes; hosting, maintenance, updates, design, development, programming and support. Always remember; "If your site cannot be located, does it really exist?

Stephen H. Sutherland
Sutherland's Web Services
www.sws.tc
Steve@sws.tc
231-929-2655

INDEX

Step-by-Step Guides To Start, Manage & Market Your Own Business

4th Printing!

How To Start & Manage Your Own Business

For anyone who is looking to start-up a new business, this *step-by-step guide* includes planning, managing, marketing and promotion.

$21.95

Soft Cover • 104 Pages
5 1/2" x 8 1/2" 0-9628759-0-2 ©1992

New!

How to Start & Manage a Home Based Business

This book provides the knowledge and tools necessary to successfully plan, design, and start up a new business in a practical way. With a step-by-step guide for planning, managing, marketing and promotion of a small business, in an easy-to-read and easy-to-understand format. The guidelines presented will help you pursue dreams of independence and financial success.

$21.95

Soft Cover • 135 Pages
5 1/2" x 8 1/2" 1-887005-11-0 © 1996

3rd Printing!

How To Start A Participative Management Program

A concise guide for small to midsize companies that is easy to read and follow *Step-by-step planning, managing and marketing of a small business* • How to empower and involve employees • Contains tools for measuring employees work environment.

$21.95

Soft Cover • 93 Pages •
5 1/2" x 8 1/2", 0-9628759 ©1992

ABOUT THE AUTHORS
Jerre G. Lewis and Leslie D. Renn are both experienced professionals concerning small business management and entrepreneurship. For more than twenty years Mr. Lewis has been involved with business education at college level and the development of a series of small business seminars. He is a Certified Education Specialist for the U.S. Small Business Administration Volunteer Counseling Program. Mr. Renn is a business owner, entrepreneur, a small business consultant, and like Mr. Lewis, is involved with college level management instruction & business seminars. He also has extensive experience in large industry administration. Mr. Lewis and Mr. Renn received bachelors and masters degrees from Michigan universities, and both work and live in northern Michigan.

TO ORDER BUSINESS PLANS

Please Remit To:

LEWIS AND RENN ASSOCIATES
10315 HARMONY DRIVE
INTERLOCHEN, MICHIGAN 49643

Business Book # _____ Title _____
Business Book # _____ Title _____

Name _____
Address _____
City _____
State _____ Zip _____

Business Book
U.S. Shipping
& Postage $ 3.00
Total _____

Business Books

Telephone 1-231-275-7287 • Fax 1-231-275-7242 • lewisjv@centurytel.
Telephone 1-480-807-9530 • Fax 1-480-830-1187 • lrenn@cox.net

2007

How to Start and Manage:

ISBN 978-1-57916-152-1	An Apparel Store Business
ISBN 978-1-57916-153-8	A Word Processing Service Business
ISBN 978-1-57916-154-5	A Garden Center Business
ISBN 978-1-57916-155-2	A Hair Styling Shop Business
ISBN 978-1-57916-156-9	A Bicycle Shop Business
ISBN 978-1-57916-157-6	A Travel Agency Business
ISBN 978-1-57916-158-3	An Answering Service Business
ISBN 978-1-57916-159-0	A Health Spa Business
ISBN 978-1-57916-160-6	A Restaurant Business
ISBN 978-1-57916-161-3	A Specialty Food Store Business
ISBN 978-1-57916-162-0	A Welding Business
ISBN 978-1-57916-163-7	A Day Care Center Business
ISBN 978-1-57916-164-4	A Flower and Plant Store Business
ISBN 978-1-57916-165-1	A Construction Electrician Business
ISBN 978-1-57916-166-8	A Housecleaning Service Business
ISBN 978-1-57916-167-5	A Nursing Service Business
ISBN 978-1-57916-168-2	A Bookkeeping Service Business
ISBN 978-1-57916-169-9	A Bed and Breakfast Business
ISBN 978-1-57916-170-5	A Secretarial Service Business
ISBN 978-1-57916-171-2	An Energy Specialist Business
ISBN 978-1-57916-172-9	A Guard Service Business
ISBN 978-1-57916-173-6	A Software Design Business
ISBN 978-1-57916-174-3	An Air Conditioning & Heating Business
ISBN 978-1-57916-175-0	A Plumbing Service Business
ISBN 978-1-57916-176-7	A Sewing Service Business
ISBN 978-1-57916-177-4	A Carpentry Service Business
ISBN 978-1-57916-178-1	A Home Attendent Service Business
ISBN 978-1-57916-179-8	A Tree Service Business
ISBN 978-1-57916-180-4	A Dairy Farming Business
ISBN 978-1-57916-181-1	A Farm Equipment Repair Service Business
ISBN 978-1-57916-182-8	A Children's Clothing Store Business
ISBN 978-1-57916-183-5	A Women's Apparel Store
ISBN 978-1-57916-184-2	A Convenience Food Store Business
ISBN 978-1-57916-185-9	A Pest Control Service Business
ISBN 978-1-57916-186-6	A Printing Business
ISBN 978-1-57916-187-3	An Ice Cream Business
ISBN 978-1-57916-188-0	A Mail Order Business
ISBN 978-1-57916-189-7	A Bookstore Business
ISBN 978-1-57916-190-3	A Home Furnishing Business
ISBN 978-1-57916-191-0	A Retail Florist Business
ISBN 978-1-57916-192-7	A Radio-Television Repair Shop Business
ISBN 978-1-57916-193-4	A Dry Cleaning Business
ISBN 978-1-57916-194-1	A Hardware Store Business
ISBN 978-1-57916-195-8	A Marine Retailing Business
ISBN 978-1-57916-196-5	An Office Products Business
ISBN 978-1-57916-197-2	A Pharmacy Business
ISBN 978-1-57916-198-9	A Fish Farming Business
ISBN 978-1-57916-199-6	A Personal Referral Service Business
ISBN 978-1-57916-200-9	A Solar Energy Business
ISBN 978-1-57916-201-6	A Building Service Contracting Business
ISBN 978-1-57916-202-3	A Retail Decorating Products Business
ISBN 978-1-57916-203-0	A Sporting Goods Store Business
ISBN 978-1-57916-204-7	A Retail Grocery Store
ISBN 978-1-57916-205-4	A Cosmetology Business
ISBN 978-1-57916-206-1	A Franchised Business
ISBN 978-1-57916-207-8	An Electronics Industry Consulting Practice Business
ISBN 978-1-57916-208-5	An Independent Consulting Practice Business
ISBN 978-1-57916-209-2	An Independent Trucking Business
ISBN 978-1-57916-210-8	An Accounting Service Business
ISBN 978-1-57916-211-5	A Nursery Business
ISBN 978-1-57916-212-2	A Seminar Promotion Business
ISBN 978-1-57916-231-9	A Bar & Cocktail Lounge Business
ISBN 978-1-57916-214-6	A Wheelchair Transportation Business
ISBN 978-1-57916-215-3	A Fertilizer and Pesticide Business
ISBN 978-1-57916-216-0	A Desktop Publishing Business
ISBN 978-1-57916-217-7	A Crime Prevention Business
ISBN 978-1-57916-218-4	A Gift Shop Business
ISBN 978-1-57916-219-1	A Handcraft Success Business
ISBN 978-1-57916-220-7	A Coin-Operated Laundries Business
ISBN 978-1-57916-221-4	A Property Management Business
ISBN 978-1-57916-222-1	An Auto Supply Store Business
ISBN 978-1-57916-223-8	A Men's Apparel Store Business
ISBN 978-1-57916-224-5	A Temporary Help Service Business
ISBN 978-1-57916-225-2	An Advertising Agency Business
ISBN 978-1-57916-226-9	A Firewood Sales Business
ISBN 978-1-57916-227-6	A Children's Bookstore Business
ISBN 978-1-57916-228-3	A Used Bookstore Business
ISBN 978-1-57916-229-0	A Sandwich Shop Deli Business
ISBN 978-1-57916-230-6	An Instant Print/Copy Shop
ISBN 978-1-57916-231-3	A Gift Specialty Store Business
ISBN 978-1-57916-232-0	A Gift Basket Service Business
ISBN 978-1-57916-233-7	A Hospitality Management Business
ISBN 978-1-57916-234-4	A Hotel Business
ISBN 978-1-57916-235-1	A Catering Service Business
ISBN 978-1-57916-236-8	A Carpet-Cleaning Service Business
ISBN 978-1-57916-237-5	A Window-Washing Service Business
ISBN 978-1-57916-238-2	An Innkeeping Service Business
ISBN 978-1-57916-239-9	An Apartment Preparation Service
ISBN 978-1-57916-240-5	A Kiosks and Cart Business
ISBN 978-1-57916-241-2	A Janitorial Service Business
ISBN 978-1-57916-242-9	A Medical Claims Processing Business
ISBN 978-1-57916-243-6	A Nursing Home Care Business
ISBN 978-1-57916-244-3	A Home Health Care Business
ISBN 978-1-57916-245-0	A Referral Services Business
ISBN 978-1-57916-246-7	A Hair Styling Salon Business
ISBN 978-1-57916-247-4	A Child Care Service Business

How-To Business Books

ISBN 978-1-57916-248-1	How to Buy and Sell A Business
ISBN 978-1-57916-249-8	How to Advertise A Small Business
ISBN 978-1-57916-250-4	How to Write A Successful Business Plan
ISBN 978-1-57916-251-1	How to Finance Your Business for the 21st Century
ISBN 978-1-57916-252-8	How to Market Your Business for the 21st Century
ISBN 978-1-57916-152-1	How to Start & Manage Your Own Business
ISBN 978-1-57916-152-1	How to Start & Manage a Home Based Business
ISBN 978-1-57916-152-1	How to Start a Participative Management Program

Library Discount - 20%
Retail Discount - 20%
$3.00 Postage & Handling
$21.95 Each
www.smallbusbooks.com

To Order Business Plans

Please Remit To:
Lewis & Renn Associates
10315 Harmony Drive
Interlochen, Michigan 49643

ISBN # _____ Title _____

ISBN # _____ Title _____

Name _____

Address_____

City _____

State_____ Zip _____

Business Book _____

U.S. Shipping & Postage **$ 3.00**

Total _____